Perhaps the greatest compliment I can pay an author is to read his book to my wife and my five children, ages eleven to seventeen. This book on prayer, written by Dr. Jim Orrick, is not the first book by him that I have read to my family. That speaks to my high regard for him and his ministry. This book on kingdom prayer is no exception. This book, so well organized as to read as a personal or family devotion, is not the musings of a young Christian minister who is overly ambitious to get himself published. Actually, it's the product—indeed, the fruit—of a man who has faithfully and as deeply as any man I know availed himself to the ordinary means of grace for five-plus decades. There is no one I know in the Christian world who has memorized more Scripture, hymns, catechisms, poems, and the like, which have all greatly benefitted his own prayer life. This is the work of a man who knows the triune God. But the genius of Orrick's work is that he can take the deepest and most profound insights that would edify the most mature of Christians and communicate those very truths in such a way that a young Christian, even one who is not yet a Christian, could understand. In other words, this book is for everyone.

– *Brian Payne,*
Senior pastor, Lakeview Baptist Church, Auburn, AL
Professor of Christian Theology and Expository
Preaching at Boyce College

Searching for great resources to disciple new believers can be like Goldilocks tasting porridge. Too difficult, and it frustrates; too fluffy, and it misleads. Jim Orrick has that much sought-after gift of taking deep truths and bringing the tray to the common man. When a book can be handed to an unbeliever for evangelism, read through with a new believer to disciple, worked through with the family for worship, and also delight the soul of the seasoned in Christ, it is a helpful book.

–*Josh Lagrange,*
Church planter

As Christians, we are a naturally sinful and forgetful people who consistently need to be reminded of the power of prayer. Following the outline of the Lord's Prayer, Jim Orrick has written a profound yet practical resource detailing seven distinct ways in which prayer sanctifies the Christian on a daily basis. *Seven Thoughts Every Christian Ought to Think Every Day* encouraged me to depend even more fully on my Father's sustaining grace in my life and ministry, and for that I am deeply thankful.

– James H. Winfrey,
Missionary mobilizer, Reaching and Teaching

Christian prayer should not feel like a performance marked by a sense of pressure and failure. Instead, it's an open invitation to speak with our heavenly Father. With his own fatherly wisdom, Jim Orrick helps us see how God gently uses prayer to change us. The book is flavored with pithy proverbs, colorful stories, and earthy illustrations that help the truth take root in our hearts. Over and over, I was refreshed and encouraged by Orrick's many insights gleaned from decades of walking closely with God.

– David Gundersen,
Lead Pastor, BridgePoint Bible Church, Houston, TX

SEVEN THOUGHTS EVERY CHRISTIAN OUGHT TO THINK EVERY DAY

SEVEN THOUGHTS EVERY CHRISTIAN OUGHT TO THINK EVERY DAY

LAYING A FOUNDATION FOR A LIFE OF PRAYER.

JIM SCOTT ORRICK

FREE GRACE PRESS

Seven Thoughts Every Christian Ought to Think Every Day: Laying a Foundation for a Life of Prayer

Copyright © 2021 by Jim Scott Orrick

All rights reserved. Written permission must be secured from the author to use or reproduce any part of this book, except for brief quotations in critical reviews or articles.

Scripture quotations are from the ESV® Bible (The Holy Bible, English Standard Version®), copyright © 2001 by Crossway, a publishing ministry of Good News Publishers. Used by permission. All rights reserved.

Scripture quotations marked KJV are from the King James Version of the Bible, public domain.

Published by Free Grace Press
1076 Harkrider
Conway, AR 72032
freegracepress.com

Cover design by Scott Schaller

ISBN: 978-1-952599-25-5 (Paperback)
978-1-952599-26-2 (Ebook)

Contents

Author's Preface ... ix

Part I

The Primary Purpose of Prayer ... 1

Why Pray? ... 2
Do You Really Want a Blank Check? ... 3
Better Than a Blank Check ... 5
Prayer Brings Us to God ... 6
The Heart of Worship ... 7
Praying in Jesus's Name ... 7
Prayer Is an Essential Daily Exercise ... 9
What God Does Not Want ... 11
What God Does Want ... 12
Why Every Day? ... 13

Part II

The Seven Thoughts ... 17

#1 We are children in the family of God. ... 19
#2 God is worthy to be worshiped. ... 29
#3 God is a good king. ... 43
#4 God is worthy to be trusted and obeyed. ... 55
#5 We are dependent on God for everything. ... 65

#6 We agree with God about sin and forgiveness.   79
#7 God is in control.   91

PART III

PRAYING IN JESUS'S NAME   105

It Does Not Mean This   105
We Are Coming to God through Christ   107
We Are Coming to God like Christ   108
A Brief Digression   109
Back to the Point   110
We Are Coming to God for Christ   111

Author's Preface

I have deliberately written this book in a simple, easy-to-understand style. Both new believers who are just beginning a life of prayer and nonreligious people ought to be able to understand it. In some sections of the book, I carefully explain how to become part of God's kingdom. I hope that this will help people who might be curious about how to become a Christian. I have also attempted to explain ideas that will benefit believers, regardless of their level of spiritual maturity, who are interested in learning how to live a more faithful life of prayer. I support every idea with Scripture, and many of the references are noted, but some Scripture passages I paraphrase or quote only briefly, and some are not noted. Again, this is part of my attempt to write in a simple, uncluttered style.

Each of the chapters is broken down into seven subsections identified by headings of *Day 1*, *Day 2*, and so on. The best way to make your way through the book is to carefully read one of the sections each day. If you do this, you will read through the entire book in less than two months. Every day, turn into prayer the information you have read that day.

Part I

The Primary Purpose of Prayer

Since God has already formed a perfect and unalterable plan, why should we pray?

God answers prayer. There are times when he acts because someone has asked him to act, and his being asked was a condition of his acting. He told Solomon that he would grant his request for wisdom "because you have asked," and the Lord added, "Behold, I now do according to your word" (1 Kings 3:11–12). The Holy Spirit says, "You do not have, because you do not ask" (James 4:2). God answers prayer.

At the same time, God has an unchangeable eternal purpose. He has formed this purpose according to his own will, and for his own glory he has absolutely and minutely planned everything that happens. In other words, God has a secret, sovereign will that cannot fail. He has planned everything that has happened, he has planned everything that will happen, and there is no possibility that his plan will alter. This being the case, how could God answer prayer? Does he ever change his mind and make a new plan? No one can present God with information he has not already known. Your Father in heaven knows what you need before you ask him. No one can formulate a plan of action better than the one already made by "God only wise" (Rom. 16:27 KJV). If God is going to do everything that he has planned, and he has foreordained whatsoever comes to pass, then what is the point of our praying?

Why Pray?

Several good answers can be proposed to the question of why we should pray, but we will consider three here. First, God has commanded us to pray. We must never allow a theory about God's sovereignty—even if it is the right theory—keep us from doing our plainly revealed duty. We are to live according to God's revealed will, not according to his secret will. His secret will may be the rock of our comfort, but his revealed will is the rule of our conduct. "He has entrusted us with his commands but not with his decrees."[1] He has commanded us to pray, so we are to pray. Suppose a little child is doing a task his father has told him to do, and someone asks him, "Why are you doing that?" The child may not understand why his father has commanded him to do what he is doing, but he gives an adequate answer when he says, "Dad told me to do this." The first reason we pray is simple: "Father said so."

A second reason for praying is that God has not only planned what will happen but he has also planned the means of bringing about what will happen, and one of those means is our prayers. A farmer may pray, "Lord, please bless me with a good crop this year," but what does he do next? He plants the seeds. Only a lazy farmer would say, "If God has sovereignly decreed for me to have a good crop, then he will make the fields spontaneously produce it, and I do need not to plant anything." A lazy man will not plow because the sky is cloudy. A lazy Christian will not pray because God is sovereign. God has not only planned the end, he has also planned the means of bringing about the end. He answers prayers because he has planned to answer prayers.

These are two excellent reasons to pray: God has commanded us to pray, and God has planned to answer our prayers. Both answers deserve deep consideration, but in this book, I intend to focus on the third and chief reason for praying: Because prayer changes us.

---

1 William Jay, *Morning Exercises for Every Day in the Year* (Harrisonburg, VA: Sprinkle, 1998), 147.

Do You Really Want a Blank Check?

Before we home in on the idea that the primary purpose of prayer is that prayer changes us, take a moment to consider this question: Do you really want God to give you everything you ask for? Do you want him to hand you a signed blank check? Suppose God were to say to you, "You may plan every detail of the rest of your life, including when and how you are going to die. I will give you a year to think about how you want to live the rest of your life, and at the end of the year, you are to write out your plan. You may consult anyone you like to help you to choose wisely. I will see to it that your plan is carried out exactly as you devise it." Would you do it?

Before you say yes, think back over your life and remember some of the foolish, harmful things you once wanted with all your heart: perhaps a binding relationship with a person who proved to be a scoundrel, a job that might have trapped you in the wrong career, possessions that would have distracted you from more important pursuits, pleasurable experiences that would have led to sin, and so on. What if you had been able to write out your life plan when you deeply wanted those things? Your plan certainly would have included many of the things you now see would have been terrible for you.

Not only that, but think back on some of the things you craved and fought for and eventually attained. Were those things as satisfying when you possessed them as they were alluring when you were pursuing them? "No thing we grasp proves half the thing we crave."[2] "All things that are, are with more spirit chased than enjoyed."[3] Did you ever imagine at the time when you were panting and pining for the thing you craved that a time would come when you would have no interest at all in your darling obsession?

---

[2] Christina Rossetti, "Heaviness May Endure for a Night, but Joy Cometh in the Morning," in *A Sacrifice of Praise*, ed. James H. Trott (Nashville: Cumberland House, 2006), 559.
[3] William Shakespeare, *The Merchant of Venice*, act 2, scene 6, lines 12–13.

> Enjoy'd no sooner but despised straight,
> Past reason hunted, and no sooner had,
> Past reason hated as a swallow'd bait
> On purpose laid to make the taker mad.[4]

Are you sure you are wiser now—wise enough to plan out the rest of your life? Can you imagine how far astray your life would be today if God had allowed you to formulate an unalterable detailed plan for your life while your desires were aflame with unholy passions? Sometimes the most severe punishment God administers is giving a person exactly what he or she longs for.

On the other hand, think of an unpleasant event that happened to you that you did not want to happen. Perhaps you prayed earnestly that it would not come about, but God allowed it and blessed you through it. In fact, you now see that the blessing would not have ensued without the unpleasant event. The dark clouds you so dreaded were, in fact, heavy with rains of mercy,[5] and you now must admit that the gloom was, after all, "shade of his hand, outstretched caressingly."[6] You now say, "Before I was afflicted I went astray, but now I keep your word," and "It is good for me that I was afflicted, that I might learn your statutes" (Ps. 119:67, 71).

Similarly, I can think of decisions I made that proved to be of momentous significance in my life, but at the time, I was completely unaware I was making a life-changing decision. Had I been making a detailed plan for my life, I would surely have left out the day I made the seemingly insignificant decision that turned out to be a momentous one. Robert Frost describes a walk in the woods where he chose one path over another for the mere reason that the path he took was covered with leaves and therefore seemed to be less used. But the consequences of that choice were far-reaching:

---

4 William Shakespeare, "Sonnet 129," lines 5–8. The entire sonnet is on the disappointment of worldly pleasures.
5 William Cowper, "God Moves in a Mysterious Way," 1774.
6 Francis Thompson, "The Hound of Heaven," 1893.

> I shall be telling this with a sigh
> Somewhere ages and ages hence:
> Two roads diverged in a wood, and I—
> I took the one less traveled by,
> And that has made all the difference.[7]

"The Spirit helps us in our weakness. For we do not know what to pray for as we ought, but the Spirit himself intercedes for us with groanings too deep for words" (Rom. 8:26). Apparently, the Spirit also intercedes for us with plans too profound for us to imagine.

Better Than a Blank Check

Jesus said, "Ask, and it will be given to you; seek, and you will find; knock, and it will be opened to you. For everyone who asks receives, and the one who seeks finds, and to the one who knocks it will be opened" (Matt. 7:7–8). I suspect that many people read this promise and think that the Lord is offering us the opportunity to do what we have just recognized would be foolish to attempt. They think he is saying, "Here is a signed blank check. Fill it in with whatever you want." That is not what he means. What *does* he mean then? Jesus continued, "Or which one of you, if his son asks him for bread, will give him a stone? Or if he asks for a fish, will give him a serpent?" (vv. 9–10). Jesus teaches that our loving Father in heaven gives us what we ask for when we ask for what is good. What if the son asks for a stone or a serpent—or the wrong job or the wrong wife or the wrong diagnosis? Will a good father give bad gifts? "If you then, who are evil, know how to give good gifts to your children [and withhold bad gifts from them], how much more will your Father who is in heaven give good things to [and withhold bad things from] those who ask him!" (v. 11). God is good; therefore, we do not get everything for which we unwisely ask, seek, and knock.

> Not what we wish, but what we want [lack]
> O let Thy grace supply.

---

7 Robert Frost, "The Road Not Taken," 1915.

> The good, unasked, in mercy grant;
> The ill, though asked, deny.[8]

There are times, however, when we wisely ask, seek, and knock for something good, and our Father says to us what he said to Solomon: "Behold, I now do according to your word" (1 Kings 3:12). Those prayers are granted without fail. Perhaps we do not see how they are granted, but we make two mistakes in our interpretation of the Lord's promise about answered prayer. One, we do not allow that our request may be granted in eternity. Two, we do not recognize that our requests are being answered by the way God uses our praying to shape our character. In this case, you might say that while we may not obtain the things we ask, seek, and knock for, we become persons who are shaped by what we ask, seek, and knock for. We are shaped by our prayers, and this shaping is surely the primary purpose of prayer.

Prayer Brings Us to God

Imagine you are in a small boat that is just a few feet offshore. You want to get the boat to land. The boat is tied to a tree on the shore, so you pull on the rope. Which moves—the land or the boat? It is the boat that moves and not the land, but no matter, the result is the same. The boat and the land are together.[9] "If God does not by his providence give us what we desire, yet, if by his grace he makes us content without it, it comes much to one."[10]

The great goal of prayer is not to change God's thinking but to bring ourselves to God's way of thinking—to make our will conform to his. Why would we want to change the will of a perfectly wise God who loves us as a father? Everyone who is born

---

8 James Merrick, "Eternal God, We Look to Thee," 1763.
9 Adapted from William Jay, *Evening Exercises for Every Day in the Year* (Harrisonburg, PA: Sprinkle, 2004), 338.
10 Matthew Henry's comment on God's denying Moses's request to enter the promised land but allowing him to see it from Mount Pisgah (Deut. 3:21–29). On the same passage, Henry notes, "God may accept our prayers, and yet not grant us the very thing we pray for." *Matthew Henry's Commentary on the Whole Bible in Six Volumes* (New York: Fleming H. Revell, n.d.) 1:739.

again into God's family has said in his heart, "God knows best. I will trust him." Christian growth is the process of bringing all our thoughts, all our desires, and all our actions into complete agreement with that initial conviction: "God knows best. I will trust him."

The Heart of Worship

Prayer is the heart of true worship. God prescribed to Israel many rituals and activities that they were to offer him in worship. There were various sacrifices and feasts and pilgrimages to Jerusalem and the temple, which was the focal point of performing what God had prescribed. But the goal of all these activities was prayer. During his final days on earth, Jesus went to Jerusalem and cleansed the temple. "And he was teaching them and saying to them, 'Is it not written, "My house shall be called a house of prayer for all the nations"? But you have made it a den of robbers'" (Mark 11:17). The Father's house was and is to be a house of prayer. When the Lord indwells us as believers, we become his living temples, and we are to each become a house of prayer. The sacrifices we bring to God in his temple are spiritual sacrifices: "The sacrifices of God are a broken spirit; a broken and contrite heart, O God, you will not despise" (Ps. 51:17). "Through [Jesus] then let us continually offer up a sacrifice of praise to God, that is, the fruit of lips that acknowledge his name" (Heb. 13:15). The incense we offer is the incense of prayer: "And another angel came and stood at the altar with a golden censer, and he was given much incense to offer with the prayers of all the saints on the golden altar before the throne, and the smoke of the incense, with the prayers of the saints, rose before God from the hand of the angel" (Rev. 8:3–4). Christian worship is our bringing our thoughts, affections, and actions into conformity with God's revelation of himself in Christ, and this is the essence of true prayer.

Praying in Jesus's Name

God has revealed himself through Jesus Christ. Both in his deeds and in his words, Jesus revealed God. After he returned to heaven,

Jesus sent his Holy Spirit to further explain his actions and teachings. The Holy Spirit of Jesus moved holy men to write down what he was teaching them, and the Spirit guided these holy men to accurately record in brief books and letters what they had learned from him. God preserved those accurate records in the books of the New Testament. Now the only worship that God accepts is the worship offered by people who are thinking about him the way he has revealed himself through Jesus. "Whoever does not honor the Son does not honor the Father who sent him" (John 5:23). When we pray, we are under the influence of Jesus's work and teaching, and we think of God as Jesus has revealed him. We aim to pray as if Jesus himself were in our situation. This is what it means to pray in Jesus's name.[11] The Father receives worship only from those people who esteem and love and reverence him in accordance with the way the Son taught. Jesus declared, "I am the way, and the truth, and the life. No one comes to the Father except through me" (John 14:6). We must think about all things and people the way Christ has taught us to think about them. We must feel toward all things and people the way Christ has taught us to feel. We must act concerning all things and people the way Christ has taught that God's children ought to act. Jesus was so accurate in communicating God's will to us that he asserted, "Whoever has seen me has seen the Father" (John 14:9).

If Christian worship is our conforming our thoughts, affections, and actions to God's revelation of himself through Christ, and if Jesus says that the heart of worship is prayer, then it follows that the primary purpose of prayer is not that we change *God's* mind but that we change *our* minds, conforming our minds to his.

Prayer is the rope that connects our boat to God. When we pray, we pull the rope. The great goal of prayer is accomplished not when our confused, imperfect will is done but when we know, obey, and submit to God's will. When we pull on the rope of prayer, God does not move; we move. But the effect is the same:

---

11 What it means to pray in Jesus's name is explained more extensively in the final chapter of this book.

we become united with God. We become "partakers of the divine nature" (2 Peter 1:4).

Prayer Is an Essential Daily Exercise

I played basketball and ran track in my college years. Athletic scholarships paid for much of my education. During those years, it was essential for me to stay in top physical condition, so I regularly worked out for hours a day. After graduation, when other responsibilities in life demanded my attention, I no longer had the time to cultivate the same level of fitness I had maintained in college. I did, however, want to stay in good shape physically, so I began taking a walk every morning. It was not much, but it was something. That daily walk afforded the bare minimum of exercise I needed to maintain basic health. Sometimes I'd be able to work out more vigorously later in the day, but if not, at least I had done the essential daily exercise. I still take a twenty-minute walk virtually every day.

Many Christians consistently spend hours a day in prayer. Most of us do not, however, and God probably does not expect it of us. But all of us must pray. An essential minimum of praying is required if we are to stay in healthy spiritual condition. How much is the minimum? The question is not "How little can I get by with?" The questions are "What does the Lord expect?" and "What do I need to stay spiritually healthy?"

Some people seem to almost enjoy being sick. When you ask them how they are doing, they will never say they are fine. I am not sure what their standard of wellness is, but they certainly don't seem to reach it. They would feel guilty if they admitted they were doing well. Maybe they do feel bad all the time, and perhaps there is nothing they can do about it. But I suspect that a healthy diet, regular sleep habits, and a twenty-minute walk every day would make a lot of unhealthy people feel much better.

Apparently, some Christians have grown accustomed to constantly being slightly sick spiritually. Ask them how their prayer life is, and they will inevitably say that it is not what it ought to be. They would feel guilty if they said, "My prayer life is just fine." After all, there is always room for improvement. Is this constant sense of inadequacy an inevitable attendant of humility? Is a constant sense of sickness an indicator of spirituality? Is this what the Lord expects of us? Does he expect us to continually be in a state of unease about our prayer life? Or could it be that we continually feel inadequate because we have unrealistic or even ungodly expectations of what is required to maintain a healthy prayer life? What does God expect? What do we need?

When his disciples asked the Lord Jesus to teach them to pray, he began his brief answer with a slightly abbreviated version of what is commonly called the Lord's Prayer.[12] This is not Jesus's only instruction about praying. For example, as part of his answer to the disciples' question on this very occasion, he tells a story to emphasize the importance of persistence in prayer. But he begins his lesson with an amazingly simple and brief model of prayer. The Lord's Prayer can be recited in under thirty seconds, speaking at a normal pace. Praying the Lord's Prayer may take longer than merely reciting it, but still, it is brief. It is as if the Lord is saying, "You do not have to pray for hours in order to pray well."[13]

Now, Jesus himself would sometimes spend all night praying, and we might well assume that the forty days of fasting in the wilderness were days saturated with prayer, so there are surely times when any follower of Christ will devote extended times and seasons to concentrated prayer. Some Christians are called to lives of prayer and intercession; this may be their main ministry. They are like college athletes on scholarship and must pray long and

---

12 This exchange is recorded in Luke 11:1–4. The full version of the Lord's Prayer is found in Matt. 6:9–13.
13 While I am heartily convinced of the truth of what I write in this paragraph, brief praying must not be sloppy, hurried praying. Consider well what Alexander Whyte wrote: "I am as certain as I am standing here, that the secret of much mischief to our own souls, and to the souls of others, lies in the way that we stint, and starve, and scamp our prayers, by hurrying over them. Prayer worth calling prayer; prayer that God will call true prayer and will treat as true prayer, takes far more time, by the clock, than one man in a thousand thinks." Quoted in *Giant Steps*, ed. Warren Wiersbe (Grand Rapids: Baker, 1981), 204.

hard. But not everyone is called to that type of ministry. What is the spiritual equivalent to my twenty-minute walk? What is the absolutely essential praying that God expects of us and that we need to maintain spiritual health? The answer: the Lord's Prayer.

What God Does Not Want

Before he taught us the Lord's Prayer, Jesus warned against several wrong ideas about what constitutes a healthy prayer life. First, he tells us to beware of praying to impress people: "And when you pray, you must not be like the hypocrites. For they love to stand and pray in the synagogues and at the street corners, that they may be seen by others. Truly, I say to you, they have received their reward. But when you pray, go into your room and shut the door and pray to your Father who is in secret. And your Father who sees in secret will reward you" (Matt. 6:5–6). Do you measure the health of your prayer life by what would impress others if they knew about it? We may not be tempted to stand up in the middle of a church service and start praying aloud or drop to our knees in the middle of the street, but we can still be praying to impress other people. We may want people to know how much we pray. We may want them to catch us on our knees in prayer. We at least want to impress ourselves. Jesus tells us that we must choose whether we will pray to the god who sees in public or to the God who sees in secret. We cannot pray to both. They are different gods.

Jesus warns us as well against praying with the idea that we will impress God by using a lot of meaningless phrases: "And when you pray, do not heap up empty phrases as the Gentiles do, for they think that they will be heard for their many words. Do not be like them, for your Father knows what you need before you ask him" (Matt. 6:7–8). The idea behind using a lot of empty phrases is that it helps us to pray a long time, and praying a long time will move God to do what we ask. But God does not want long, meandering prayers full of meaningless phrases. No wonder. Do you like it when a preacher takes an hour to say what he might have said in twenty minutes? Would you like it if a child stood before you and mindlessly repeated the same request over and over? "Mommy, I want a cookie. Mommy, I want a cookie. Mommy, I want a cookie. Mommy . . ." You get the idea. We ourselves cannot pay attention to our own prayers when we pray like that. If we cannot pay attention to our prayers, why ought we to expect that God will pay attention to them?[14] God is not a stone. He listens to us. He is our Father. He is not like a dryer in a laundromat that requires just a few more quarters to get the job done. He does not need us to impress him with how long we can keep up meaningless chatter. "Be not rash with your mouth, nor let your heart be hasty to utter a word before God, for God is in heaven and you are on earth. Therefore let your words be few" (Eccl. 5:2).

Neither does he need us to inform him of every detail of our request. He knows what we need before we ask him. Granted, there is nothing too insignificant for us to bring before our Father, and the problem with too many of us is that we are spending far too little time in prayer. But it is a fundamental misconception that a healthy prayer life consists in our trying to impress God with the length or the minute details of our prayers.

What God Does Want

God does not want us to draw near to him with our lips while our hearts are far from him. True prayer requires the engagement of our hearts—that is, our thoughts—and God uses prayer to teach us to think like him. The Lord wants us to always keep several key thoughts in mind—thoughts that he wants us to think every day. These fundamentally important thoughts or ideas are, not surprisingly, summarized in the Lord's Prayer. As mentioned earlier, what is commonly called the Lord's Prayer might more accurately be called the *Model Prayer*, since Jesus is using it to teach us how to

---

[14] George Herbert asks this same question in a very thought-provoking poem in which he explores the reasons for unanswered prayer. See Jim Scott Orrick, ed., "The Method," in *A Year with George Herbert* (Eugene, OR: Wipf and Stock, 2011), 105.

pray. It is like an outline for us to use when we pray. There is nothing wrong with simply repeating the prayer exactly as it appears, as long as we do not repeat it with our lips while our heart is far away. The primary purpose of the prayer, however, is to teach us how to pray. Jesus says, "Pray like this." Why? Because these are the issues God is most interested in. You are children of God. In praying for these issues, you are deliberately harmonizing your thoughts and desires with your Father's thoughts and desires. These are thoughts you ought to think every day.

Why Every Day?

One of the petitions in the Lord's Prayer is "Give us this day our daily bread." This petition makes it clear that the Lord intended that we ought to pray like this every day. Every day we should think certain thoughts and pray certain petitions. Why every day? If the principles of Christianity are so obviously true, and if a sinful course of living is so obviously false, then why must Christians constantly remind themselves that it is so? Why the ongoing, lifelong struggle to pursue holiness and shun evil?

We need daily reminders of the truth because we live in a world that has been successfully attacked by a highly intelligent enemy who has been permitted to dominate the world of ideas—that is, Satan has corrupted the thinking processes of the human race. Before the Lord saved us, Satan blinded our minds to keep us from seeing the light of the gospel of the glory of Christ (2 Cor. 4:4), and spiritual truth seemed foolish to us (1 Cor. 2:14). Believers are now living in a hostile world surrounded by a population whose minds have been corrupted so that they have forgotten they are eternal beings created in the image of God. Consequently, they live as if the world of three dimensions is the only world there is and as if this world is the only one they will ever inhabit.

Humans are fundamentally social creatures who were created to be influenced by one another. We learn to speak the language of those in our environment. We accept as normal the culture into which we are born and reared. We naturally accept the values of that culture, and we look at the world using the eyes of that culture. We want to fit in. We want the approval of those around us.

Christ has come and told us that our beloved native culture is corrupt. Its values are wrong; its way of looking at the world is wrong. He teaches us another way of thinking, and he has set up a counterculture based on truth. Under the influence of his Spirit, we believe him and accept him as our Prophet, Priest, and King, but there remains in us a liability to be persuaded by those around us. This is a fundamental characteristic of humans, whether redeemed or not. Furthermore, the language of the corrupted world is our native language, and that culture is our native culture. There remains in us something that says, "That is my culture, and those are my people."

A recovering alcoholic may need to remind himself every day that drunkenness is bad and sobriety is good. Something powerful in him still yearns for the stupor of alcohol, but he must be governed by a higher, nobler principle. We would not discourage such a man by telling him that if sobriety were such a good thing, he would not need to fight so hard for it every day. Similarly, we are recovering sinners. Every day we are tempted to slip back into the world's way of thinking, which is our old, native way of thinking. So, the Holy Spirit exhorts us, "I appeal to you therefore, brothers, by the mercies of God, to present your bodies as a living sacrifice, holy and acceptable to God, which is your spiritual worship. Do not be conformed to this world, but be transformed by the renewal of your mind, that by testing you may discern what is the will of God, what is good and acceptable and perfect" (Rom. 12:1–2). He also says, "But exhort one another every day, as long as it is called 'today,' that none of you may be hardened by the deceitfulness of sin" (Heb. 3:13). Again, the Lord exhorts us to "put off your old self, which belongs to your former manner of life and is corrupt through deceitful desires, and to be renewed in the spirit of your minds, and to put on the new self, created after the likeness of God in true righteousness and holiness" (Eph. 4:22–24). This process of conforming our thinking to God's way of thinking requires us to faithfully utilize all the means the Lord has appointed for us to train ourselves for godliness (1 Tim. 4:7). This book is devoted to how the Lord uses prayer to give us the mind of Christ (1 Cor. 2:16) and transform us into his image (2 Cor. 3:18).

The world around us says, "You are one of us, and this is how we think." In the Lord's Prayer, the Lord reminds us believers, "You are no longer a child of the world; you are now part of my family, and this is how we think. These are seven thoughts you ought to think every day."

Part II

The Seven Thoughts

Our Father in Heaven

Thought #1

We are children
in the family of God.

DAY 1

You are a child of God.

You are a child of God; now act like it. Once you were an enemy to God. You were hostile to him. Thoughts of God made you uncomfortable. But God loved you and reconciled you to himself at great cost. "God shows his love for us in that while we were still sinners, Christ died for us" (Rom. 5:8). He made you more than a servant in his house; he made you a child in his family. He adopted you. Now accommodate yourself to the family.

Perhaps you know of a loving family who adopted a child who turned out to be a rebel. The mother and father did all they could to make the adopted child feel loved and wanted. But the child, instead of responding to the parents with gratitude and appreciation, began to rebel against them. He broke the rules of the house. He constantly disrupted family peace. He tried to influence the other children to disagree with the parents. Do not be that kind of child.

On the other hand, we have seen families adopt a child out of poverty or out of an abusive situation, and the child responds with gratitude and appreciation. The child sees that he has been given a golden opportunity to live a healthy, productive life filled with love. He respects his parents. He joyfully cooperates with the family philosophy. Every day he remembers his old life, and he knows that his life is different now because of his parents. He is thankful. Be that kind of child.

DAY 2

Our Father gives life.

Throughout history, about one half of humans have not survived childhood.[1] You did. In fact, every single one of your ancestors

---

[1] Max Roser, "Mortality in the past—around half died as children," Our World in Data, June 11, 2019, https://ourworldindata.org/child-mortality-in-the-past.

lived to be old enough to become a parent. You are no accident. In a swirling snowstorm of death, God sheltered your family so that you might one day be born and grow up to know him.

When you were born, you did not know God. You had a nature that was predisposed to be preoccupied with anything other than God. We "were by nature children of wrath, like the rest of mankind" (Eph. 2:3). I came from an earnest, sincere Christian family, and I went to church and heard the Bible. I was even baptized and became a member of a good church, but I did not love God. I was afraid of God. I feared that if I gave myself entirely to him, he might ruin my life. I did not trust him. Neither did you. We were separated from God and dead in our trespasses and sins.

But God made us alive. He showed us the futility of our ways and the emptiness of our lives without him. He taught us to grieve over our sins and to hate them. He enabled us to turn away from our sins and turn to him with the full intention of obeying him. He opened our blinded eyes and enabled us to see Jesus as the Savior perfectly suited to our needs. Though we may have formerly thought little of Jesus, God made it possible for us to see Jesus with fresh appreciation and admiration. We saw Jesus to be trustworthy, and we trusted him. We believed in him, for God had given us the new birth. God gave us the ability to see and feel and want to enjoy the invisible things of God. But most of all, he gave us the desire to see and feel and enjoy the invisible God. Our Father gave us life.

Day 3

Our Father provides.

We do not have to be anxious. When we are worried and anxious, it indicates that we are not trusting our Father to provide us with what we need. We may cast all our cares upon him because he has undertaken the task of caring for us (1 Peter 5:7). He who watches over his people neither slumbers nor sleeps (Ps. 121:4). There is no need for both of us to stay awake through the night. So, he gives sleep to his beloved.

Our Lord directs us to consider the birds of the air and the flowers of the field (Matt. 6:26–30). God feeds the birds and clothes the flowers of the field, and he does it without their fretting. We are more valuable than birds and flowers. What kind of father would feed the birds and let his children starve?

Do you worry and fret because you have made your happiness depend on getting and maintaining more than food and clothing? Let us be content with those (1 Tim. 6:8). Are you worried and upset because people do not appreciate all you are doing? "Martha, Martha, you are anxious and troubled about many things, but one thing is necessary. Mary has chosen the good portion, which will not be taken away from her" (Luke 10:41–42). Choose to live a life of simple devotion to God. Do not fill your life with unnecessary distractions. The distracting, trivial thing you choose to do crowds out the focused, meaningful thing you might have done. Do not worry and fret. Your Father in heaven will provide for you.

> Said the robin to the sparrow,
> "I should really like to know
> Why these anxious human beings
> Rush about and worry so."
> Said the sparrow to the robin,
> "Friend, I think that it must be
> That they have no heavenly Father
> Such as cares for you and me."[2]

It must be a frightening experience to be born. We leave the warm, dark, wet womb and enter the cold, bright, dry outside world. But, ah, that soft comforting voice that we heard while we were still in the womb speaks gently to us, and she holds us close and kisses us. And the strong hands belonging to that other familiar voice take us and hold us against his strong chest. It must have

---

2   Elizabeth Cheney, "Overheard in An Orchard."

been soothing. Something inside us whispered, "There is someone looking after you. All will be well."

> O Lord, my heart is not lifted up;
>   my eyes are not raised too high;
> I do not occupy myself with things
>   too great and too marvelous for me.
> But I have calmed and quieted my soul,
>   like a weaned child with its mother;
>   like a weaned child is my soul within me.
> O Israel, hope in the Lord
>   from this time forth and forevermore. (Psalm 131)

Day 4

Our Father loves us.

Those who think that faith is an easy thing to gain have surely never tried to get it.[3] Faith is a persuasion of the truth based on testimony. The most important truths are not explained; they are revealed. They are not deciphered but are believed. Of all God's revealed truth, faith stands gasping and groping for support when it looks up at the vast mountain of this truth: God loves us.

God loves you. This is a sentence so often on the lips of those who would persuade others to follow Christ. But the way it trips so glibly out of their mouths, I wonder if they have any idea what they are saying. And the way it falls dull on our ears and drops to the floor with a thud while we pick up some toy of the earth shows that we do not hear it, much less believe it.

What is love? There are different kinds of love. When you were an enemy to God, he was delighted at the prospect of doing you good. That is love. It is love with a good will, or *benevolent* love.

---

[3] "They surely have never made the trial who imagine that it is an easy thing to believe." Jay, *Morning Exercises*, 438.

Benevolent love is not merely the determination to do someone good; the *delight* of doing him good must also be present. The person described in 1 Corinthians 13:1–2 was doing many right things, but something essential was missing. It was not missing in God's benevolent love for you. In saving you, he was not simply doing a merciful thing; he showed mercy to you because he loved you. He did not love us because we were lovely or worth loving. We were without strength. His strong, saving love for us is a great mystery that defies explanation. What was said of God's love of Israel may be said of his love for us: God loves you because he loves you.

A second kind of love God has for his redeemed children is his love for us because he is pleased with us. This is love with pleasure, or *complacent* love. God loved us when we were unlovable, but by his grace we are transformed into people that he finds lovely. He not only loves you as a poor, pitiful thing that needs help; he loves you as a child who brings him pleasure. He likes you. How could it be otherwise if we are being transformed into the likeness of his Son? If we have the mind of his Son? If we have the Spirit of his Son? He is working in us that which is pleasing to him. If he loved us when we were his enemies and we hated him, now that we are his children and we love him, will he not love us? Without faith it is impossible to please God. With faith it is possible to please him.

God is not angry with you, his child. If you believe in Jesus, then God's wrath toward you is appeased. His anger was spent on Jesus when he stood in your place. God loves you.

Child of God, you may be poor, but you have God's love. You may feel lonely, but God loves you and is with you. You do not have anything that God needs, but he wants you to be near him because he loves you. Gaze into the smiling face of your Father and say, "Whom have I in heaven but you? And there is nothing on earth that I desire besides you. My flesh and my heart may fail, but God is the strength of my heart and my portion forever" (Ps. 73:25–26).

Oh, Lord, I believe. Please help my unbelief.

DAY 5

Our Father is in heaven.

God is not your equal. He is vastly superior to you. He is your Father who is *in heaven*. He loves you with delighted goodwill and approval. We love him with delighted admiration. But merely to say that God is admirable is like saying Beethoven was a pretty good songwriter or that Jonathan Edwards was fairly bright. Any admiration of God that falls short of worship is an insult.

Your Father is in heaven, so fear him. Yes, fear him so that you do not sin presumptuously. Fear him so that you do not incur his displeasure. Fear him because he disciplines those he loves. Fear him because the fear of the Lord is the beginning of wisdom. Do not make the mistake of thinking that God is altogether such a one as you are. Fear him because he delights in those who fear him. Fear him because he sends his angels to encamp around those who fear him and delivers them.

Fear him, yes, but fear him with the loving, tender respectful fear that is due to a father. He is your Father in heaven, so you do not have to explain every detail to him. He is your Father in heaven, so he has power to help you. He is your Father in heaven, so he sees what is done in secret.

Keep the two ideas in equipoise. He is your Father, so you may draw near to him boldly. He is in heaven, so you must draw near to him in holy reverence and fear.

DAY 6

As children of God, we have both privileges and responsibilities.

If God is your father, then that makes you his child. You are a child of God. There is a time for acknowledging your sin and mourning over it, but as you enter God's presence in prayer, remember that

Jesus taught us to say, "Our Father." There are times to remember that God is your creator and to praise him for it. There are times to joyfully submit to God as your master and as the judge of all the earth and as the sovereign, solitary, Supreme Being. But however frequently or infrequently you think of God in these important ways, every day you are to remember that God is your Father and you are his child. At least once a day "enter his gates with thanksgiving, and his courts with praise! Give thanks to him; bless his name! For [your Father] is good; his steadfast love endures forever, and his faithfulness to all generations" (Ps. 100:4–5).

There are privileges that come with being God's child. You may come boldly to the throne of grace. A little girl whose daddy is the president of the company does not need an appointment to see her daddy. It is likely that she will not even knock before she rushes into his office with her broken doll or her broken heart. Her daddy will understand. He will be glad to see her. You have that kind of access to your Father in heaven. He is glad to see you. No problem is too small to bring to him. No joy is too trivial to thank him for it. Like a mother looking into the eyes of her nursing baby and singing him a joyful song, so your Father will rejoice over you with joy and singing; "he will rest in his love" (Zeph. 3:17 KJV).

Responsibilities come with being God's child. You are the child of a noble, worthy Father. Live nobly and in a way worthy of your calling. Your Father is the God of truth; live truly. Your Father is holy; be holy. He is light; walk in the light. The people around you will learn what your Father is like by listening to you and watching you. "Let your light shine before others, so that they may see your good works and give glory to your Father who is in heaven" (Matt. 5:16).

Day 7

You are not alone. You are part of God's family.

We address God as *our* Father, not *my* Father. You are not the only child in the family. You have brothers and sisters. They are interested in the same important things that you are. You are not alone. Your brothers and sisters will help you, and you are to look out for ways you can help them.

How can you help one of your brothers or sisters today? You may be able to pray with someone today. You certainly can pray *for* someone today.

Do not foster the idea that no one loves you and no one understands you. Elijah felt like he was the only one who knew and loved God, but he was wrong. God had seven thousand followers in Israel. It may be that they were too secretive and ought to have made themselves known to Elijah. But they were in hiding because they were afraid of Ahab and Jezebel. Perhaps you feel lonely like Elijah, but you are not alone. Perhaps a brother or sister around you feels like Elijah, and you need to make yourself known. Are you the one who is hiding? God has children all over the world, and it is likely that some of those children are near you. Find them and become an encouragement to them. When you encourage others, you yourself will be encouraged.

Jesus said, "Who are my mother and my brothers?" "My mother and my brothers are those who hear the word of God and do it" (Mark 3:33; Luke 8:21).

HALLOWED BE YOUR NAME

THOUGHT #2

God is worthy
to be worshiped.

Day 1

God's name is his character.

When the authors of the Bible write of God's name, they are referring to his revealed character, not merely the word by which he is designated. God has used a variety of words to designate himself. There are some general terms like *God* and *Lord* and *The Power*, and there are specific terms like *Yahweh*, *Jehovah Jireh*, and *Jesus*, to give just a few examples. We call these specific terms *proper nouns*. God's name includes all these general terms and proper nouns, but it is more than any one of them. It is all of them and more. God's name is more than a word, and it is more than a proper noun; it is what ought to come to mind when we think of him. God's *name* is who he is.

When you first meet someone, you may be introduced to him and learn that his name is Bill, but initially, you know almost nothing about Bill the person. You may even have trouble remembering that his name is Bill. At first, he may be no more than *that tall guy*. But if you grow to know Bill better, his name accrues meaning. Soon, when you hear the name *Bill*, you think of what you have come to know about him. If he becomes your friend, you learn about his personality. You accumulate memories together. You share joys and sorrows. When you first met, the proper noun *Bill* meant nearly nothing to you; it was just the word used to designate this yet unknown person. But after years of friendship, his name, Bill, triggers a multitude of thoughts—thoughts of love and appreciation. As the friendship continues, ideas associated with the person named Bill become more fully developed in your mind, and your appreciation for him grows deeper. You do not sit around and meditate on the word *Bill*, but you have learned to know his character and his ways. You have learned Bill's name in the biblical sense.

This is how it is with the name of your Father in heaven. At first, God may have seemed distant. He was near, but you were far. Even when you were not interested in him, he was watching over you and protecting you. Even when you were his enemy, he loved you. At the right time, he called you to himself. You came to him, and he began to reveal his character to you. He had given you a heart to know him, and you wanted to know him more. He came to the door of your life, and he said to you, "Behold, I stand at the door and knock. If anyone hears my voice and opens the door, I will come in to him and eat with him" (Rev. 3:20). He invited you to his presence, and he said, "Ask, and it will be given to you; seek, and you will find; knock, and [the door] will be opened to you" (Matt. 7:7; Luke 11:9). You have taken him at his word. You knocked, and he opened the door, and you entered his presence with thanksgiving in your heart; you entered his courts with praise. You have come to know his character—his name—and you say, "There is none like you. Your name is set apart from all others. Your name is hallowed, and it deserves to be hallowed by me and by others. May it be so." You ought to think this every day.

Day 2

We hallow God's name when we glorify him in all the ways he makes himself known.

Hallowed is not a word we use or hear often. It is possible that the only other place you have read it is in Abraham Lincoln's Gettysburg Address. Lincoln gave his renowned speech at a ceremony dedicating part of the Gettysburg battlefield to be a cemetery for fallen soldiers. After acknowledging that it was a fitting and proper thing to do, Lincoln said, "But, in a larger sense, we can not dedicate—we can not consecrate—we can not hallow—this ground. The brave men, living and dead, who struggled here, have consecrated it, far above our poor power to add or detract." Before the fields of Gettysburg became battlefields, they were farm fields. Crops grew there. Cattle grazed there. Then those common farm fields became special because of the bloody battle that took place there. After that, soldiers who survived the battle could never again see those fields merely as good farmland. Families of the fallen would view those fields and remember their loved ones who fought and died there. To this day, visitors to Gettysburg feel the solemnity of the place as we remember what happened on that soil, and we are moved to reverence and admiration. It is not a place for making jokes; flippancy is out of place there. It has been set apart as special; it has been forever distinguished from other fields; it has been hallowed.

There was a time when God's name did not move you to reverence and admiration. You knew nothing about his character—his name. Perhaps you even treated his name with flippancy, or you thought that the true God was no different from the gods of other religions. Now that God has revealed himself to you, you want to think of him with respect and reverence. You admire him, and you want others to admire him. You want his name to be hallowed.

The opposite of hallowing God's name is to take his name in vain. Something is vain when it is useless or when it is unimportant or ineffective. Likewise, when we take God's name in vain, we are acting like his character is unimportant or ineffective. Taking God's name in vain is more than unnecessary swearing or using God's titles in a meaningless way. Taking God's name in vain does include using God's names and titles in a flippant, meaningless way, but it means more than that. It also means that we ignore him or act as if he has not revealed himself in his Word, his ordinances, and all his works. We take God's name in vain when we live most of our lives as if God did not exist.

We hallow God's name when we glorify him in all the ways he makes his character known. In our hearts we regard him with a special respect, a special admiration, a special love, and we worship him alone. We hallow God's name when we go beyond merely speaking respectfully about him—when we do more than just act like we respect him. We hallow God's name when we draw near to him in our hearts.

What Lincoln said about the Gettysburg battlefield is true of our attempts to hallow God's name. We cannot make God's name any more hallowed than it already is. But we can recognize his character in the various ways that he makes himself known. Perhaps we can also help others see God and hallow his name.

Day 3

We hallow God's name when we fear him.

Several times in the Bible, the Holy Spirit describes true religion as *the fear of the Lord*. For example, "The fear of the Lord is clean, enduring for ever" (Ps. 19:9), and "The fear of the Lord is the beginning of knowledge" (Prov. 1:7). The Lord required the kings of Israel to make for themselves a handwritten copy of God's law and commanded that each "shall read in it all the days of this life, that he may learn to fear the Lord his God" (Deut. 17:19).

Fear is a sense of uneasiness we feel in the presence of someone or something that has the power to hurt us or make us unhappy. We naturally want to avoid persons and situations that make us afraid. So how can God require us to fear him and at the same time require us to draw near to him? The two requirements seem antithetical to one another, but they are, in fact, complementary. If we were to pet a lion, we would experience a sense of awe that differs from what we might experience in petting a kitten.

When we fear God, we are thinking of him with profound respect, and that respect enhances our appreciation of his grace. Our fear of God makes us feel the wonder of his love and mercy for us. When we fear God, we feel what an honor he shows us by revealing himself to us as "a God merciful and gracious, slow to anger, and abounding in steadfast love and faithfulness, keeping steadfast love for thousands, forgiving iniquity and transgression and sin." For he also is the one "who will by no means clear the guilty, visiting the iniquity of the fathers on the children and the children's children, to the third and the fourth generation" (Ex. 34:6–7).

We fear God, yet we love him and want to be near him. This holy fear and love balance and refine one another. Our fear of God keeps our love from becoming mushy sentimentality. God is not a kitten. Our love for God keeps our fear from becoming repelling terror. In *The Lion, the Witch, and the Wardrobe*, when Lucy finds out that Aslan is a lion, she wants to know if he is safe. "'Safe?' said Mr. Beaver, 'don't you hear what Mrs. Beaver tells you? Who said anything about safe? 'Course he isn't safe. But he's good. He's the King, I tell you.'"[1] God may be compared to a wild lion (and he often is in the Bible), but he is a wild lion who is on our side. In Revelation 5:5 Jesus is described as "the Lion of the tribe of Judah," and in the very next verse John sees him as "a Lamb standing, as though it had been slain." In Psalm 2, the Holy Spirit describes this balance of fear and love: "Serve the LORD with fear, and rejoice with trembling. Kiss the Son, lest he be angry, and you perish in the way, for his wrath is quickly kindled. Blessed are all who take refuge in him" (vv. 11–12). Note the same balance between fear of God and confidence in God in the following words of our Lord:

> I tell you, my friends, do not fear those who kill the body, and after that have nothing more that they can do. But I will warn you whom to fear: fear him who, after he has killed, has authority to cast into hell. Yes, I tell you, fear him! Are not five sparrows sold for two pennies? And not one of them is forgotten before God. Why, even the hairs of your head are all numbered. Fear not; you are of more value than many sparrows. (Luke 12:4–7)

If we do not fear God, everything is a threat to us. If we fear God, we need fear nothing else.

---

1 C. S. Lewis, *The Lion, the Witch, and the Wardrobe*, The Chronicles of Narnia (New York: Harper Collins, n.d.), 146. We get a similar idea in Book 1, Canto 3 of Edmund Spenser's *Faerie Queene*, when a wild lion protects Una, the heroine of the story.

Day 4

We hallow God's name when we admire him.

We seem to have an innate capacity to recognize and appreciate beauty. This capacity is a manifestation of God's image in human beings. He surely enjoys beautiful things, and he has made us so that we too may enjoy beauty. Creating us with this love of beauty is an expression of his goodness to us. He made us capable of appreciating beauty, and then he filled the world with beautiful things. Among all the creatures of the earth, only humans deliberately create beauty for the sake of beauty and admire beauty simply because it is beautiful. A spider's web pearled with the dew of a misty autumn morning may be beautiful to us, but the spider did not construct it to be a thing of beauty. Certainly, a fly does not find it to be beautiful. No doubt your dog has above-average intelligence; see if you can get your dog to appreciate the spider's web. The most intelligent animal never gazes in wonder at the stars or listens enraptured to a symphony. Sadly, neither do most humans, but we are capable of it. We recognize beauty, and we long to experience it.

When we fear God, we show respect for his great power. When we admire God, we show appreciation for his great beauty. God's character—his name—is beautiful.

What makes something beautiful? That is not an easy question to answer, but when we find something or someone to be beautiful, that thing or person appeals to us—we feel an attraction to experience the beauty. Beautiful things give us pleasure, and they give us most pleasure when we can experience them the way they were meant to be experienced. We do not want merely to see a picture of beautiful scenery—we want to feel the cold mountain air, see the tiny flowers above the tree line, and smell the sage. We want to taste the salty ocean, hear the sea gulls, and feel the sand beneath our bare feet. We want to hear the whippoorwills in the woods, take shelter from the rain beneath an overhanging rock, and smell the fragrance of the wet forest. We want to feel the cool mist of the waterfall. We want to eat the golden honey oozing from the honeycomb, mixed with melted butter on a hot flaky biscuit. We do not want just to study about composers and to read the notes of music; we want to hear "Clair de Lune." We want to finger the silky ears of a basset hound puppy. We want to sigh, close our eyes, and feel the warmth and quiet joy of rocking a baby to sleep.

When we appreciate and experience beauty, the image of God in us says, "This is the way it is supposed to be; this approaches perfection." When we see the beauty of God's character—his name—the image of God in us says, "This is perfection. This is what you were made to enjoy." And we want to experience him. The Holy Spirit says to us, "Oh, taste and see that the LORD is good!" (Ps. 34:8). David says, "One thing have I asked of the LORD, that will I seek after: that I may dwell in the house of the LORD all the days of my life, to gaze upon the beauty of the LORD and to inquire in his temple" (Ps. 27:4). We hallow God's name when we admire his beauty and seek to enjoy him.

DAY 5

We hallow God's name when we love him.

As important as it is to fear God and admire him, we must go further. If we are to hallow his name as he deserves, we must love him. A man once asked Jesus, "Which commandment is the most important of all?" Jesus answered, "The most important is, 'Hear O Israel: the Lord our God, the Lord is one. And you shall love the Lord your God with all your heart and with all your soul and with all your mind and with all your strength'" (Mark 12:28–30).

Without love, all else we offer to God is worthless. Are you pleased with loveless gifts from someone who ought to love you? God does not need anything we have. He says, "If I were hungry, I would not tell you, for the world and its fullness are mine" (Ps. 50:12). The only reason he values anything we offer him is because we offer it in love, and our Father is pleased with our little gifts and prayers to him when we offer them because we love him.

My daughters' homemade cards for me are among my favorite gifts. A couple of my daughters have developed into unusually fine artists, but when they first started drawing and making cards for me, no one else would have thought that their work was very good. But I did. I put their cards up on the refrigerator, and then I put them into a box reserved especially for their cards. I treasure that box full of homemade Father's Day cards and birthday cards. In some of the pictures you can barely tell the difference between "Mommy," "Daddy," and the dog. But I think they are great because they were given to me in love. When one of my daughters was about four years old, she gave me her only dollar tied up with a pink ribbon. It is one of the best gifts I have ever received. I felt like David must have felt when his men broke through enemy lines to bring him a drink from Bethlehem's well. When we love God and offer him our little talents and services, we honor him, and he is pleased. If we do not love him, nothing we offer him pleases him.

You cannot make yourself love God. You cannot make yourself love anyone, for you cannot work directly on your affections. You must work on your affections indirectly through your mind. Learn more about God's name. As you learn more about God's character, your confidence in him will be strengthened, and your love for him will grow. You will hallow his name.

Since loving God is the most important commandment, we ought to make loving God and cultivating love for God the principal effort of our lives.

DAY 6

We hallow God's name when we worship him.

When we worship God, we are expressing to him our fear, admiration, and love for him. Worship reveals that we have recognized who God is and who we are in relation to him. "You are God, and I am not, and I am happy with this arrangement."

Worshiping God enhances our enjoyment of him. When we love someone, we feel new joy when we express our love to them. Love is not fulfilled until it is expressed. It is the same when we love God. We want to tell him; we want to worship him. When we know his name, we long to express our delight in him. Sometimes we feel like our love for God is flowing over like a fountain.

Love for God is not always overflowing in our souls, however. Sometimes we feel dry and passionless toward God. These dry times are opportunities to hallow God's name and pray that we might hallow him for who he is and not just for the gifts he gives. How does a rich man know who his friends are? Similarly, if God never sent dry times into our lives, how would he know—ah, he knows all things—how would *we* know that we love him for who he is, that is, for his name?

Is God pleased when we hallow his name by worshiping him even when we do not feel like it? Perhaps that is the time when he is most pleased with our worship because that is when it is most motivated by faith and evidence of faith. Faith is believing what God has said and consequently obeying him—especially when the only reason for believing and obeying is because God has said it. When you worship God even though your soul is cast down, are you just faking it? When a baby bird who has not yet learned to fly sits on the edge of the nest and flaps its wings, is it faking it, or is it getting ready to fly? You were made to worship God. Christ has redeemed you, and the Holy Spirit has called you so that you might worship God. Your soul has wings; fly to God.

Day 7

When we hallow God's name, we want him to be glorified by all persons and in all things.

Like sunshine streaming in through a sparkling clean window, the glory of God's name beams brightly through his clean, holy children. We were not always clean and holy, but "Christ loved the church and gave himself up for her, that he might sanctify her, having cleansed her by the washing of water with the word, so that he might present the church to himself in splendor without spot or wrinkle or any such thing, that she might be holy and without blemish" (Eph. 5:25–27).

Between 1508 and 1512, Michelangelo painted the ceiling of the Sistine Chapel. After nearly five centuries, the paintings were darkened by soot from candle smoke. When we observed the paintings, most of us simply assumed that Michelangelo had originally painted his masterpiece using subtle, subdued colors. But late in the twentieth century, the paintings were restored, and the centuries of candle soot were wiped away. What a colorful surprise lay underneath! Michelangelo had used bright, vibrant paint, and it was only the grime that made the work look so somber. Michelangelo was revealed. In our salvation, God is wiping away the grime of sin to reveal the vibrant colors of his artwork restored to its original splendor. He created us in his image, but sin distorts us. Sin distorts us, but Christ restores us. We gaze on his beauty, and we are transformed into his likeness. "And we all, with unveiled face, beholding the glory of the Lord, are being transformed into the same image from one degree of glory to another. For this comes from the Lord who is the Spirit" (2 Cor. 3:18). We become "partakers of the divine nature" (2 Peter 1:4). In his creation and restoration of humans, God is revealed.

We want others to join with us in hallowing God's name. He is worthy of all the honor of all the world. God has the wisdom and the power to dispose all things to his own glory, and we pray for this when we pray, "Hallowed be thy name." He can even overrule the evil acts of evil men to glorify his name. Joseph told his brothers, "You meant evil against me, but God meant it for good" (Gen. 50:20). Evil men crucified Jesus, but God meant it for good (see Acts 2:23). God can superintend all circumstances so that his children receive benefit and glorify his name. "We know that for those who love God all things work together for good, for those who are called according to his purpose" (Rom. 8:28).

Above all, God glorifies his name in the revelation of his character:

> Moses said, "Please show me your glory." And [God] said, "I will make all my goodness pass before you and will proclaim before you my name 'The Lord.' And I will be gracious to whom I will be gracious, and will show mercy on whom I will show mercy." (Ex. 33:18–19)

> The Lord passed before him and proclaimed, "The Lord, the Lord, a God merciful and gracious, slow to anger, and abounding in steadfast love and faithfulness, keeping steadfast love for thousands, forgiving iniquity and transgression and sin, but who will by no means clear the guilty, visiting the iniquity of the fathers on the children and the children's children, to the third and the fourth generation." And Moses quickly bowed his head toward the earth and worshiped. (Ex. 34:6–8)

Moses saw God's glory in God's name.

Your Kingdom Come

Thought #3

God is a good king, and he has all power to reign. We want him to exercise his power and extend his reign.

Day 1

We want God to subdue us to himself.

We want God to extend his reign, and we want him to start with us. At its heart, sin is the idea that we can rule ourselves better than God can rule us. Sin is rebellion against the reign of the King. Sin came into this world through disobedience to the King, and sin persists through the idea that we do not have to listen to God nor obey him. When we were children and one of our siblings tried to tell us what to do, we defiantly protested, "You are not the boss of me." When we say that to God, we are cooperating with the great rebellion instigated by Satan.

Sin has invaded the human race like a deadly virus. One of the worst things about sin is that it corrupts a person and makes him a sinner. Sin brainwashes us and causes us to embrace the philosophy of the rebellion. A person who lies becomes a liar. A person who steals becomes a thief. A person who rebels becomes a rebel.

Mercury is a heavy metal that exists in a liquid state. Years ago, it was commonly used in thermometers as the liquid that would rise and fall, indicating the temperature. It is extremely dangerous because when it enters the human body through the skin, it can cause severe health problems or even death. I once saw a boy playing with a drop of mercury about the size of a raisin, rolling it around on the palm of his hand. We had no idea how dangerous it was. Playing with sin is like playing with mercury—it does not merely get on our hands; it permeates the surface of our lives and enters our system and corrupts us. All disobedience to God is rebellion, and no matter what attempts we may make to serve God, all our efforts are meaningless as long as we are living in rebellion against the King: "Has the LORD as great delight in burnt offerings and sacrifices, as in obeying the voice of the LORD? Behold, to obey is better than sacrifice, and to listen than the fat of rams. For rebellion is as the sin of divination, and presumption is as iniquity and idolatry" (1 Sam. 15:22–23).

Sin is the attempt to overthrow the rightful King. Sin is a declaration that we prefer a king other than God. It is a vote cast in favor of another king—ourselves.

When we pray, "Thy kingdom come," we are laying down our arms of rebellion. We are asserting our loyalty to the rightful King. We bow before his throne, saying, "Reign over me."

DAY 2

Jesus is the King.

God has always been the King of the universe, but when Jesus commenced his public ministry, he said, "The time is fulfilled, and the kingdom of God is at hand; repent and believe in the gospel" (Mark 1:15). Something new was about to happen. God was getting ready to turn over to Jesus the right to rule the earth.

Since the fall, God had allowed sin to reign over most of the earth, but when the time was fulfilled, God sent his Son, Jesus, to quell the rebellion and reclaim the earth for God. This required that the eternal Son of God become man. Sin had entered the human race and the reign of righteousness in humanity was overthrown through one man's disobedience. Therefore, sin had to be defeated and the reign of righteousness reestablished through one man's obedience. When the holy and just God determined to forgive sinful rebels, it had to be done in a manner consistent with his holiness and justice. God could not simply pretend that the rebellion had not occurred. God's holy character and law had declared that the wages of sin is death, so if God were to pardon sinners, then a substitute must suffer the prescribed penalty of death. God the Son was appointed to be the substitute for sinners. Since the eternal Son of God cannot die, he became a man who could die so "that through death he might destroy the one who has the power of death, that is, the devil" (Heb. 2:14). God the Son joined his perfect divine nature with the human nature of Jesus of Nazareth and became the God-man: two natures in one person.

Jesus won a resounding victory over Satan on the cross. He redeemed his people from God's wrath "by canceling the record of debt that stood against us with its legal demands. This he set aside, nailing it to the cross. He disarmed the rulers and authorities and put them to open shame, by triumphing over them in him" (Col. 2:14–15).

After dying on the cross, Jesus "was declared to be the Son of God in power according to the Spirit of holiness by his resurrection from the dead" (Rom 1:4). He said, "All authority in heaven and on earth has been given to me" (Matt. 28:18). He returned to heaven in his resurrected human body where "he sat down at the right hand of the Majesty on high" (Heb. 1:3). "God has highly exalted him and bestowed on him the name that is above every name, so that at the name of Jesus every knee should bow, in heaven and on earth and under the earth, and every tongue confess that Jesus Christ is Lord to the glory of God the Father" (Phil. 2:9–11).

The kingdom has come. God is now reigning through Jesus the King.

Day 3

We pray that Satan's kingdom may be destroyed.

If the kingdom has already come, then why do we pray, "Thy kingdom come"? Because although the King has been enthroned, widespread resistance to the King still remains. This resistance is under the direction of Satan, God's hateful, evil enemy.

The Bible is not clear about how Satan came to be Satan, but God created him, for God created all things. Although God had the power to have stopped him, he allowed Satan to tempt the first humans into sinning against God. Since Adam, the first man, had been appointed by God to stand as a representative for the human race, when Adam sinned, all mankind descending from him in the normal, biological way sinned in him and fell with him in his first sin.[1] Satan is the mastermind behind this sinful rebellion, and he successfully convinced humans to embrace the fundamental principle of his rebellion, which, again, is insistence on self-rule. Because all humans are born with a predisposition to embrace the principles of the rebellion, we are by nature the children of wrath and followers of Satan, even though we may strongly deny that we are following him. Since humanity, the world, was plunged into sinful ways of thinking and living, Satan became the prince, or ruler, of this world.

On the cross, Jesus dealt Satan a crushing blow. Just after our first parents had sinned, God said to the serpent, "I will put enmity between you and the woman, and between your offspring and her offspring; he shall bruise your head, and you shall bruise his heel" (Gen. 3:15). When Jesus was crucified, he fulfilled this ancient prophecy. On the cross, Satan bruised Jesus's heel, but Jesus bruised Satan's head. Sometimes people say that Satan is alive and well, but this is not entirely accurate. He is alive, but he is not well: his head has been bruised.

Just before his crucifixion, Jesus anticipated the coming battle with Satan, and he said, "Now will the ruler of this world be cast out" (John 12:31). Satan, like a strong man, had seized power over the peoples of the earth. His house was full of miserable slaves to sin. The Son of God became man so "that through death he might destroy the one who has the power of death, that is, the devil, and deliver all those who through fear of death were subject to lifelong slavery" (Heb. 2:14–15). "But no one can enter a strong man's house and plunder his goods, unless he first binds the strong man. Then indeed he may plunder his house" (Mark 3:27). On the cross, Jesus bound the strong man, and ever since then he has been delivering slaves out of Satan's house and making them sons and daughters of God. When we pray, "Your kingdom come," we are praying that Satan's kingdom will be destroyed.

---

1 Since Jesus was conceived by the power of the Holy Spirit in the womb of the Virgin Mary and did not descend from Adam in the ordinary way, his human nature was not sinful.

Day 4

We pray that the kingdom of grace may be advanced.

Christ has established a kingdom of grace. Under Satan's rule, sin increased, "but where sin increased, grace abounded all the more, so that, as sin reigned in death, grace also might reign through righteousness leading to eternal life through Jesus Christ our Lord" (Rom. 5:20–21). When Christ came, God opened the gates of grace to the entire world and announced that "God so loved the world, that he gave his only Son, that whoever believes in him should not perish but have eternal life" (John 3:16). Jesus proclaimed, "The Spirit of the Lord is upon me, because he has anointed me to proclaim good news to the poor. He has sent me to proclaim liberty to the captives and recovering of sight to the blind, to set at liberty those who are oppressed, to proclaim the year of the Lord's favor" (Luke 4:18–19).

Throughout history, there had always been people who knew the true God and worshiped him, but according to the Bible, nearly all of them were from the tiny nation of Israel. God's kingdom of grace was very small. It was like a tiny trickle of grace dripping in the desert. But God had promised, "I will pour water on the thirsty land, and streams on the dry ground; I will pour my Spirit upon your offspring, and my blessing on your descendants. They shall spring up among the grass like willows by flowing streams" (Isa. 44:3–4). When Christ had finished his work on earth, he returned to heaven and sent the Holy Spirit. Then the floods of grace came.

> On the mount of crucifixion,
> Fountains opened deep and wide;
> Through the floodgates of God's mercy
> Flowed a vast and gracious tide;
> Grace and love, like mighty rivers,
> Poured incessant from above;

And heav'n's peace and perfect justice
Kissed a guilty world in love.[2]

Now the Lord Jesus cries out, "If anyone thirsts, let him come to me and drink" (John 7:37). When we pray for the kingdom of grace to be advanced, we join our voice with the Lord in saying, "Come, everyone who thirsts, come to the waters; and he who has no money, come, buy and eat! Come, buy wine and milk without money and without price" (Isa. 55:1). "The Spirit and the Bride say, 'Come.' And let the one who hears say, 'Come.' And let the one who is thirsty come; let the one who desires take the water of life without price" (Rev. 22:17).

Day 5

We pray that we ourselves and others will be brought into the kingdom of grace.

In praying for the kingdom of grace to be advanced, we pray, first, that we ourselves will be brought into it. We enter this kingdom when we are born again. Jesus said, "Unless one is born again he cannot see the kingdom of God," and "Unless one is born of water and the Spirit, he cannot enter the kingdom of God" (John 3:3, 5). We cannot give ourselves the new birth any more than we gave ourselves our first birth. God must give us a new heart. The Holy Spirit describes this process in Ezekiel 36:25–27: "I will sprinkle clean water on you, and you shall be clean from all your uncleannesses, and from all your idols I will cleanse you. And I will give you a new heart, and a new spirit I will put within you. And I will remove the heart of stone from your flesh and give you a heart of flesh. And I will put my Spirit within you, and cause you to walk in my statutes and be careful to obey my rules."

If you are not yet a loyal subject in God's kingdom, pray earnestly that God will give you the new birth. If you are already

---

2 William Rees, "Here Is Love, Vast as the Ocean."

cheerfully submitting to the reign of King Jesus, give glory to God, and "rejoice that your [name is] written in heaven" (Luke 10:20).

Once we ourselves are in God's kingdom, we want God to bring others into it as well. We desire for others to see and enjoy the beauties of our King. We say, "Oh, magnify the Lord with me, and let us exalt his name together" (Ps. 34:3). We see our lost friends and loved ones living as if the world of physical things is the only world there is while they are neglecting their everlasting souls, and we pray that they might hear and feel the Lord asking, "What does it profit a man to gain the whole world and forfeit his soul?" (Mark 8:36).

Because we want the kingdom of grace to be advanced, we are willing to do our little part to advance it. We "pray earnestly to the Lord of the harvest to send out laborers into his harvest" (Matt. 9:38). When we hear "the voice of the Lord saying, 'Whom shall I send, and who will go for us?' [we say,] 'Here am I! Send me'" (Isa. 6:8). We gladly and generously give our money and our time for the advancement of the kingdom of grace.

Day 6

We pray that the kingdom of glory may be hastened.

One day, Satan's kingdom will be destroyed. One day, the last of God's sheep will be gathered into the fold. The last of God's Noahs will be brought into the ark. The sun will set on the long "today" of the kingdom of grace, and the day will dawn "when the Lord Jesus is revealed from heaven with his mighty angels in flaming fire, inflicting vengeance on those who do not know God and on those who do not obey the gospel of our Lord Jesus. They will suffer the punishment of eternal destruction, away from the presence of the Lord and from the glory of his might, when he comes on that day to be glorified in his saints, and to be marveled at among all who have believed" (2 Thess. 1:7–10). Christ "will appear a second time, not to deal with sin but to save those who are eagerly waiting for him" (Heb. 9:28). Are you eagerly waiting for him? "When the Son of Man comes, will he find faith on earth?" (Luke 18:8). Will he find faith in you?

I grew up in a house that was always clean, but it usually looked "lived in." If I came home from school and the newspaper was not on the coffee table, there were no dirty dishes on the counter, all the books were off the floor, and a freshly prepared dessert was on the kitchen table, I would be sure to ask, "Are we expecting someone?" If someone should look into your daily life, would that person ask, "Are you expecting someone?" Every day we make choices as to how we spend our time and what we think about. Do these choices indicate we are expecting Jesus's return and longing for him to come back?

When we pray, "Your kingdom come," we pray that this kingdom of glory will be hastened. We pray that we will be found faithful. We pray that God will make us ready to live in the kingdom of glory.

DAY 7

We pray that God will make us ready to live in the kingdom of glory.

The greatest evidence that you and I will one day be happy in the kingdom of glory is that we are now being prepared to live there.[3] There will be no sin in the kingdom of glory. Do you hate sin and fight to get it out of your life? Everyone in the kingdom of glory will be a follower of Jesus. Do you seek out and enjoy the company of Jesus's followers now? Everyone in the kingdom of glory will delight in God's Word. Do you delight in God's Word

---

[3] "If he has, by the agency of his Holy Spirit, fitted you in the temper of your soul for the world of glory, you may be assured that he designs you for it. If you bear the image of the heavenly, you will partake of their condition. If you have the dawn of that blessed state, you will have the day. Grace is of the same nature with glory; they differ only in the degree" (William Jay, *Morning Exercises*, 439).

now? Everyone in the kingdom of glory will love God. Do you love God now?

Eternal life begins in us while we are still in our bodies on earth. For "this is eternal life, that they know you the only true God, and Jesus Christ whom you have sent" (John 17:3). Merely saying that Jesus is Lord will not get you to heaven; you must receive Christ as Lord and do the will of God. Jesus said, "Not everyone who says to me, 'Lord, Lord,' will enter the kingdom of heaven, but the one who does the will of my Father who is in heaven. On that day many will say to me, 'Lord, Lord, did we not prophesy in your name, and cast out demons in your name, and do many mighty works in your name?' And then I will declare to them, 'I never knew you; depart from me, you workers of lawlessness'" (Matt. 7:21–23). The very first step in doing God's will is to believe in Jesus. "Then they said to him, 'What must we do, to be doing the works of God?' Jesus answered them, 'This is the work of God, that you believe in him whom he has sent'" (John 6:28–29). Through believing in Jesus, we are forgiven of our sins. "He saved us, not because of works done by us in righteousness, but according to his own mercy, by the washing of regeneration and renewal of the Holy Spirit" (Titus 3:5). When the Holy Spirit regenerates and renews us, we do not become sinless, but he begins to make us holy—we must be made holy, or we will not enter heaven, for without holiness, no one will see God (Heb. 12:14). We were not saved by our good works, but we become zealous for good works. We are "waiting for our blessed hope, the appearing of the glory of our great God and Savior Jesus Christ, who gave himself for us to redeem us from all lawlessness and to purify for himself a people for his own possession who are zealous for good works" (Titus 2:13–14). "Blessed are the pure in heart, for they shall see God" (Matt. 5:8). If today the kingdom of glory is in you, one day you will be in the kingdom of glory. "He who testifies to these things says, 'Surely I am coming soon.' Amen. Come, Lord Jesus!" (Rev. 22:20).

Your Will Be Done

Thought #4

God is worthy to be trusted and obeyed.

DAY 1

God is wise and good, so we trust him.

I remember well the sobering experience. I was a young boy, maybe nine or ten years old, and I was on my knees attempting to pray. I was using the Model Prayer as my guide, and the prayer seemed to be proceeding smoothly until I came to this petition: "Thy will be done on earth as it is in heaven." I paused before saying it and thought about what I was about to do. I was about to tell God that he could do whatever he wanted to do in my life. I thought what a rash and dangerous thing it would be to give God permission to do such a thing. I considered the possibilities: *What if he did not want me to be a professional baseball player? What if he wanted me to be a missionary living in a mud hut? What if he wanted me to marry an unattractive woman?* I felt the temptation to merely mouth the words "Thy will be done," and get through the prayer, but I knew that God would know my insincerity. I would be lying to God if I said it but never meant it. I could not say it. I did not trust God. All cheerful, voluntary submission is founded on trust.

When we pray that God's will may be done, we recognize the necessity of obedience, but *trust* must come before true obedience. This petition is rooted in the confidence that God is wise and God is good. The absolute best thing that can happen to us and to this world is that God's will be done on earth as it is in heaven.

DAY 2

We value God's will over our own will.

When we are reluctant to know God's will, to obey God's will, or to submit to God's will, we are revealing something about ourselves. We value someone else's will more than we value God's will. That someone else is nearly always ourself. We prefer our will over God's will.

Every deliberate sin grows out of the belief that we know better than God. We think we are better able to discern the benefits of an action or thought. We may consider the consequences of our sinful action and convince ourselves that the satisfaction we will get from our sin outweighs the consequences we may have to endure. We may even convince ourselves that God does not want us to be unhappy, and we will surely be unhappy if we fail to get our way, so it must be God's will for us to get our way. When we sin, we are saying, "I am—at least in this instance—a better, wiser person than you are, God."

Whether a sin is deliberate or undeliberate, every sin comes out of a heart that objects to God's absolute rule. Our sinfulness is essentially a protest against God's sovereignty.

When God adopts us into his family, he changes our hearts. We recognize that before he changed us, we were in rebellion against his will. We regarded him with distrust and suspicion. But he revealed himself to us in Christ: Christ suffering and dying for sinners; Christ offering to reconcile us to God. God showed us his love in Christ, and we believed him. We trusted him. We received Christ. We now want his will to be done even when it means that our desires will not be done. But if we want his will to be done, and we conform our will to God's will, then when God does his will, he is also doing what will ultimately please us too. "Delight yourself in the Lord, and he will give you the desires of your heart" (Ps. 37:4).

> With eager heart and will on fire
> I strove to win my great desire.
> "Peace shall be mine," I said; but life
> Grew bitter in the barren strife.
>
> My soul was weary, and my pride
> Was wounded deep; to Heaven I cried
> "God grant me peace, or I must die;"
> The dumb stars glittered no reply.

Broken at last, I bowed my head,
Forgetting all myself, and said,
"Whatever comes, thy will be done;"
And in that moment, peace was won.[1]

Day 3

God reveals his will in creation, providence, conscience, and the Bible.

God has revealed to us what he wants us to think and believe. He has told us what he wants us to do. This is his *revealed* will. God makes his will known in the works of creation and in providence, as well as in our consciences, but he most clearly reveals his will for us in his Word, the Bible.

In creation and providence, God reveals that he is powerful—he rules over storms and brings the seasons. He reveals that he is good—he created us capable of enjoying pleasures and then filled the earth with pleasurable things and experiences. God reveals in our consciences that he is holy. He reveals that we are moral beings, knowing right and wrong, and he makes it known that he will judge us.

Creation and providence and conscience show enough of God's will to make every person know there is a God and teach us that we have not always obeyed his revealed will. Creation and providence and conscience show us that we are not right with God, but they cannot show us how to get right with God. God has revealed his will for our salvation in the Bible. There God teaches us about his Son, Jesus, and all that he has done to reconcile us to God. In the Bible, God reveals all that we must believe and do so that we might know him and please him.

If we desire to know and obey God, we must pay attention to God's creation and providence as well as our conscience, but we

---

[1] Henry Van Dyke, "Peace," *The Poems of Henry Van Dyke*.

must give special attention to his Word, the Bible. It is not enough that we know God's will; God's will is to be done.

Day 4

We must submit to God's secret will.

In addition to his revealed will, God also has a *secret* will. He has an eternal purpose, which he formulated in eternity past. He foreordained everything that comes to pass. His secret will includes the salvation of his elect, the unfolding events of history, and the time of the final judgment. God's secret will even includes sinful acts committed by humanity and how he will use these for his ultimate glory.

A sinful act is a violation of God's revealed will, but in his mysterious wisdom, God uses sins to help bring about his secret will or plan. For example, when we crucified Jesus, it was a wicked, sinful act—a flagrant violation of God's revealed will. At the same time, God had planned for Jesus to be crucified. It was part of his secret will. "This Jesus, delivered up according to the definite plan and foreknowledge of God, you crucified and killed by the hands of lawless men" (Acts 2:23). Similarly, Joseph's brothers disobeyed God's revealed will when they sold Joseph into slavery, but they were fulfilling God's secret will. Joseph told them, "You meant evil against me, but God meant it for good, to bring it about that many people should be kept alive, as they are today" (Gen. 50:20).

There are times when people may behave sinfully toward us and we cannot do anything about it. At other times we must endure seasons of sadness or sickness. It is perfectly legitimate to use lawful means to escape these unpleasant circumstances, but if we must endure them, we are to endure them patiently and without complaining against God. These things are part of his secret will for us, and we pray that God will enable us to submit to his will in all things.

DAY 5

God's will is good.

On the evening before his crucifixion, our Lord prayed, "My Father, if it be possible, let this cup pass from me; nevertheless, not as I will, but as you will" (Matt. 26:39; see also Luke 22:42). God allows us the same privilege as Jesus: we may pray for the removal of trials. But we are required to make the same concession as Jesus: we want God's will to take precedence over our own.

We must trust God when we first turn over our lives to his sovereign will. If, however, we are to know true peace, we must learn to say continually, "Whatever comes, your will be done." The main purpose of our lives is to conform our thinking and our actions to God's will.

This does not mean we must pretend that we enjoy pain or think a bad act is a good act. God does not say that everything that happens to us is good, but "we know that for those who love God all things *work together* for good, for those who are called according to his purpose" (Rom. 8:28, emphasis added).

Sodium by itself is toxic to humans. So is chloride. But when sodium and chloride are mixed together in the right proportions, they make salt, something that is good and useful to us. This illustrates how God can take our sin, the sin of others, sickness, disasters, and other unpleasant circumstances—none of which may be good in themselves—and he can work them together for good.

DAY 6

We want to do God's will immediately, cheerfully, and completely.

We pray that God's will may be done on earth as it is in heaven. How is God's will done in heaven?

In heaven, God's will is done immediately. Delayed obedience is disobedience. Some parents give their child a command, and when the child does not obey, the parents repeat the command—maybe a little louder or more sternly. Still the child does not obey. The parent threatens, "Don't make me count to ten!" Still nothing. "One, two, three . . ." Perhaps when the parent gets to nine the child begins to obey. This type of parenting conditions the child to delay obedience until consequences are imminent. In heaven, God's will is done immediately.

In heaven, God's will is done joyfully. There is no greater joy than doing what our Father asks us to do. Joy is the companion of earnest, heartfelt exertion. Half-hearted obedience leads to half-hearted joy. There is a lot of wisdom in this children's poem:

> Work while you work,
> Play while you play,
> This is the way
> To be happy each day.
>
> All that you do,
> Do with your might,
> Things done by half
> Are never done right.[2]

Perhaps you have observed a well-trained working dog following the commands of his master. The dog may not understand the overall purpose of the work the master is doing; he is simply obeying the master's commands. He trusts his master, and he loves to have his master's approval. How happy the dog is! How much happier than an ill-trained, lazy dog with nothing to do. Praise God for giving us meaningful work to do! A wise man said, "I would rather be sick in bed than to have nothing to do."[3] A wiser man said, "No kind or degree of exertion is so much at variance with happiness as having nothing to do. Ennui is an insect that

---

2 Author unknown.
3 Seneca, quoted in Jay, *Morning Exercises*, 285.

preys upon all bodies at rest."[4] We are to be about our Father's business, and we are to do it cheerfully and heartily. "Whatever you do, work heartily, as for the Lord and not for men, knowing that from the Lord you will receive the inheritance as your reward. You are serving the Lord Christ" (Col. 3:23–24).

No quality is more important to instill in a child—or in ourselves—than that of cheerful submission to authority. Everyone who enters the kingdom of God must cheerfully submit to the will of God, and true happiness in life is dependent on our submitting to God immediately, cheerfully, and heartily.

In heaven, God's will is done completely. There are no half-finished houses in heaven. While on earth, King Jesus completed the work he was called to do. Before he breathed out his final breath, he was able to look back over the course of his life at all the responsibilities his Father had given him. The course was long and difficult and required God-like exertion and perseverance. But after reviewing all of God's will for his life on earth, Jesus could say, "It is finished."

DAY 7

Doing God's will leads to knowing God's will.

We cannot enter the kingdom of God until we say to King Jesus, "Your will be done." Furthermore, doing the will of God is the path of gaining knowledge and wisdom in the kingdom of God. Jesus said, "If anyone's will is to do God's will, he will know whether the teaching is from God or whether I am speaking on my own authority" (John 7:17).

Christianity is a religion that emphasizes the importance of knowledge and wisdom. God does not value mindless lip service. Jesus taught us, "When you pray, do not heap up empty phrases as the Gentiles do" (Matt. 6:7). Think about what you are saying.

---

4 Jay, 488.

Words without thoughts are meaningless. Ideas give rise to prayers and actions. Similarly, virtually all the epistles in the New Testament follow the same pattern: first a doctrinal foundation is established, and then the practical instructions for living are enjoined. Doing grows out of knowing.

It is, however, also true that knowing grows out of doing. God gives knowledge like a handheld lantern gives light. The lantern gives enough light to illumine the path for only a few steps, but when you walk those few steps, you can see a part of the path that was previously in the dark. You can see the next few steps as long as you are walking in the light. "In your light do we see light" (Ps. 36:9).

When we pray, "Your will be done," we must resolve, "I will do your will today. In the little circumstances of my everyday life, I will do your will." How can we honestly say we want God's will to be done on earth if we are not willing to do his will in our house?

Give Us This Day Our Daily Bread

Thought #5

We are dependent on
God for everything.

DAY 1

God must give us everything that we need.

Only God is self-existent. *Self-existent* means that he was not made by someone else, nor does he need anyone else. Everyone other than God must say, "I am what I have been made," or "I am what I have become." Only God can say, "I am that I am." Our very being is derived from God. "For from him and through him and to him are all things" (Rom. 11:36). Our life is lived in him: "In him we live and move and have our being" (Acts 17:28). Our universe stays together and functions because of him: "In him all things hold together" (Col. 1:17); "He upholds the universe by the word of his power" (Heb. 1:3). God is self-existent, and he does not need anything we have. The Lord says, "Every beast of the forest is mine, the cattle on a thousand hills. I know all the birds of the hills, and all that moves in the field is mine. If I were hungry, I would not tell you, for the world and its fullness are mine" (Ps. 50:10–12).

We are utterly dependent on God for everything we need to live. We are tiny and frail like a flower. "All flesh is grass, and all its beauty is like the flower of the field. The grass withers, the flower fades when the breath of the LORD blows on it; surely the people are grass. The grass withers, the flower fades, but the word of our God will stand forever" (Isa. 40:6–8). Our lives on earth are so brief. "What is your life? For you are a mist that appears for a little time and then vanishes" (James 4:14). With all our worry and fret we are powerless to lengthen our life. Jesus asks, "Which of you by being anxious can add a single hour to his span of life?" (Matt. 6:27).

Despite our utter dependence on God and our frail, brief existence, we can be so proud and believe we are self-sufficient. "For you say, I am rich, I have prospered, and I need nothing, not realizing that you are wretched, pitiable, poor, blind, and naked" (Rev. 3:17).

God's family has begun to learn the truth, and the truth is that we are poor, blind, sick, and sinful beggars at God's door. Poor beggars, yes, but Jesus said, "Blessed are the poor in spirit, for theirs is the kingdom of heaven" (Matt. 5:3). Blind beggars, yes, but Jesus said, "For judgment I came into this world, that those who do not see may see" (John 9:39). Sick, sinful beggars, yes, but Jesus said, "Those who are well have no need of a physician, but those who are sick. I came not to call the righteous, but sinners" (Mark 2:17).

Every human is totally dependent on God. Most do not realize it, but those in God's family know it. When we pray, "Give us this day our daily bread," we remind ourselves that we are small and God is big. We remember that we are poor but our Father is rich. We embrace the truth that our Father must give us everything we need.

Day 2

Every bite of food I have ever eaten has come from God's hand.

There have been many days that I have not prayed, "Give us this day our daily bread," but God gave the bread anyway, and I ate it. I ate it like a hog greedily eating acorns beneath an oak tree and never looking up to see where the acorns came from. It is hard to appreciate what you have never lacked. I have never gone hungry a single day in my life except when I have voluntarily done so. After those deliberate fasts, I return to eating with a fresh appreciation for God's generous provision of so much delicious food. If you are like I am and have enough food that you must moderate your diet so you do not gain excess weight, you are rich. Most people throughout history have not enjoyed such an abundance of food, and many people around the world can only dream of having the amount and variety of food that is in my house right now. I wonder if hungry Christians ever forget to pray, "Give us this day our daily bread." It is hard to appreciate what you have never lacked, and it is also hard to appreciate what you have not asked for.

Do not complain about the food God has provided. One of the sins for which God judged Israel in the wilderness was their complaining about the manna. They said, "We loathe this worthless food" (Num. 21:5). God punished them with fiery serpents. Food does not need to be fancy to be healthy and enjoyable. One of the best-tasting meals of my life consisted of one can of cold pork and beans that I ate while camping in Montana. Hunger is the best sauce. Our enjoyment of food is enhanced by where we eat it and sometimes by who prepared it and whom we eat it with. People away from home often long for a home-cooked meal. What they remember may be a just a simple meal. When I was living at home with my parents, the meal we would have most often was soup beans with cornbread, onions, and fried potatoes. My dad was a beekeeper, so we usually had good honey to go on the cornbread; sometimes we would crumble the cornbread up in a glass of milk for dessert. Nothing fancy, but oh, what I would give to sit around that table once again with my parents and my sisters and enjoy that simple meal. "Better is a dinner of herbs where love is than a fattened ox and hatred with it" (Prov. 15:17). "Better is a handful of quietness than two hands full of toil and a striving after wind" (Eccl. 4:6). We will enjoy our daily bread more when we ask our Father for it, receive it as a gift from his hand, and eat it with a quiet, thankful heart in his presence.

I look at the food on my table, and I usually see food I did not grow. Like my dad, I too am a beekeeper, so I am somewhat responsible for the honey on my table, but I did not make it. The bees made it. They could not have made it if God had not made the flowers bloom, not to mention the fact that God taught the bees how to make honey. I hunt, so I am somewhat responsible for the wild game on my table, but the animals ate food that God provided for them. I did not tend the animals. "The voice of the LORD makes the deer give birth" (Ps. 29:9). "These all look to you, to give them their food in due season. When you give it to them, they gather it up; when you open your hand, they are filled with good things" (Ps. 104:27–28).

Only God can make food grow. God must make the seeds sprout. God must send rain. God must warm the earth with his sun. If I have money, I may be able to buy food, but how did I get the money? I have a job, and I get paid, but I cannot work unless God gives me health and strength. "Beware lest you say in your heart, 'My power and the might of my hand have gotten me this wealth.' You shall remember the LORD your God, for it is he who gives you power to get wealth" (Deut. 8:17–18).

Every bite of food I have ever eaten or ever will eat has come from God's hand.

Day 3

Along with God's blessings, we need his blessing.

Once the food is on my table, I cannot eat it unless God gives me health and appetite. I have occasionally been so sick that I could not eat. I sometimes suffer from a condition that leaves me unable to taste food for months. I can eat it, but I cannot taste it. "There is an evil that I have seen under the sun, and it lies heavy on mankind: a man to whom God gives wealth, possessions, and honor, so that he lacks nothing of all that he desires, yet God does not give him power to enjoy them" (Eccl. 6:1–2). Along with God's blessings, we need *his* blessing. He can curse our blessings: "If you will not listen, if you will not take it to heart to give honor to my name, says the LORD of hosts, then I will send the curse upon you and I will curse your blessings. Indeed, I have already cursed them, because you do not lay it to heart" (Mal. 2:2). Solomon describes the sad case of a man who, although he is wealthy, "all his days he eats in darkness in much vexation and sickness and anger" (Eccl. 5:17). On the other hand, "Everyone also to whom God has given wealth and possessions and power to enjoy them, and to accept his lot and rejoice in his toil—this is the gift of God" (Eccl. 5:19).

Even if I have food and enjoy eating it, the food will do me no good unless God makes it nourish me. I do not know how to digest food. How is food transformed into fuel to energize me? How is food made into bones and muscles and blood and hair and skin and green eyes? Even if you know enough biology to explain the process of digestion and assimilation, you still cannot make it happen in your body or in anyone else's body. God must do it. "I praise you, for I am fearfully and wonderfully made. Wonderful are your works; my soul knows it very well" (Ps. 139:14).

I am breathing. I do not think about it. My heart is beating and my blood is circulating, but I do not make it happen. God does. We are dependent on him for everything.

Day 4

We need God to fill our hungry minds with the real food of his truth.

An insane person believes that what is not real is real. He may be convinced someone is watching him when no one is watching him. He may be convinced he is a famous historical figure. I once knew a mentally unstable woman who was thoroughly convinced she was married to a famous television news anchor. She had never even met the man, yet when she introduced herself, she called herself by his last name. She was insane. She believed that the unreal was real.

We are all so close to insanity. Every time you go to sleep, you go a little insane. You have a scary dream. You think it is real. Your body reacts. Your heart beats faster, and you may even perspire. Sometimes I cry out in my sleep because of a scary dream. I wake up and tell myself, "It is all right. It was only a dream." To whom am I speaking? Who is speaking? The calm voice of reason speaks to the beating heart of temporary insanity.

In some people, the voice of reason becomes weak or even silent. When this happens because of disease or old age, we say that dementia has set in. The person has lost touch with reality.

A similar sort of dementia can be self-induced through abusing drugs or alcohol. Isn't it strange that we humans voluntarily put something into our bodies that makes us temporarily insane? A major component of our being in the image of God is our capacity to reason. Instead of valuing this God-like gift, many seek every opportunity to dull or even silence the voice of reason.

Perhaps you do not struggle with the sins of drunkenness or mind-numbing drug abuse. However, sin makes us insane. There are mental disorders that cause a person to want to eat non-food substances like dirt, coal, or metal. King Nebuchadnezzar wanted to eat grass! When we are in our sinful insanity, we trade the real, substantial pleasures of holiness for the temporary, illusory pleasures of self-rule. We are eating forbidden fruit, and like a mind-altering drug, sin fills our heads with drunken, insane ideas. The voice of conscience may awaken us and sound a warning, but without the strengthening nourishment of God's truth, the voice of conscience may become weak and eventually silent. Sometimes God gives people up to sinful insanity. "Although they knew God, they did not honor him as God or give thanks to him, but they became futile in their thinking, and their foolish hearts were darkened. Claiming to be wise, they became fools. . . . Therefore God gave them up in the lusts of their hearts to impurity to the dishonoring of their bodies among themselves, because they exchanged the truth about God for a lie. . . . For this reason God gave them up to dishonorable passions" (Rom. 1:21–26). Our only hope for a restoration to sanity is the sovereign intervention of God. "God may perhaps grant them repentance leading to a knowledge of the truth, and they may come to their senses and escape from the snare of the devil, after being captured by him to do his will" (2 Tim. 2:25–26).

More than literal food, we need the nourishing, sanity-producing bread from God. "Man does not live by bread alone, but man lives by every word that comes from the mouth of the Lord" (Deut. 8:3). "Come, everyone who thirsts, come to the waters; and he who has no money, come, buy and eat! Come, buy wine and milk without money and without price. Why do you spend your money for that which is not bread, and your labor for that which does not satisfy? Listen diligently to me, and eat what is good, and delight yourselves in rich food. Incline your ear, and come to me; hear, that your soul may live" (Isa. 55:1–3).

Day 5

To eat spiritual bread, we must be spiritually alive.

Just as both your body and your mind need food, your spirit also needs food. What is your spirit? It is the part of you that may engage with God. It is in your spirit that you are most like God, for God is a spirit.

You are not a mere animal, although there is much you have in common with animals. You have a body; animals have bodies. You enjoy physical pleasure; animals enjoy physical pleasures. Like animals, you have something that makes your body live, and that life-giving thing is not the same thing as your body. It is essential to the life of your body, and seemingly your body is permeated with it, but if you were to lose an arm, this living something is not diminished by the loss of your arm.

So, what makes humans different from animals? We have been created in the image of God. Subtract everything that we have in common with the animals, and what remains is the image of God—the God who is spirit. You may have been neglecting your spirit. In fact, it is possible you are dead spiritually.

If you are dead spiritually, it does not mean you no longer have a spirit; it means that, similar to the way a dead thing is separated from living things, you are separated from the living God. Your fundamental perspective on what is important in life is so radically different from God's perspective that there is just no way you two are going to get along. You are dead to God.

I did not say, "You will never get along with God." You may get along with God if one of you changes his perspective. You are the one who must change. You must turn away from every action and every thought that disagrees with God's perspectives. Those thoughts and actions are keeping you away from the living God, and they are making you spiritually dead. You must be born again. God must resurrect you. And when you come alive, you will need spiritual food.

Do you hunger for spiritual food? It goes without saying that a dead person does not hunger. But a healthy, living person has an appetite. When God raises us from our spiritual deadness, we long for knowledge of the truth, but above all we crave nourishing fellowship with the living God. When Jesus had raised Jairus's daughter back to life, "her spirit returned, and she got up at once. And he directed that something should be given her to eat" (Luke 8:55). Eating is an indication that life has returned. After Jesus was raised from the dead and appeared to his disciples, "while they still disbelieved for joy and were marveling, he said to them, 'Have you anything here to eat?' They gave him a piece of broiled fish, and he took it and ate before them" (Luke 24:41–43). A person who has been resurrected to spiritual life is hungry for God and says, "As a deer pants for flowing streams, so pants my soul for you, O God. My soul thirsts for God, for the living God" (Ps. 42:1–2). "My soul longeth, yea, even fainteth for the courts of the LORD: my heart and flesh crieth out for the living God" (Ps. 84:2 KJV). Pray, "O God, you are my God; earnestly I seek you; my soul thirsts for you; my flesh faints for you, as in a dry and weary land where there is no water." And Lord, when you answer my prayer, "My soul will be satisfied as with fat and rich food" (Ps. 63:1, 5). "Blessed are those who hunger and thirst for righteousness, for they shall be satisfied" (Matt. 5:6). "Oh, taste and see that the LORD is good!" (Ps. 34:8).

DAY 6

Jesus is the Bread of Life.

In the Bible verses quoted at the end of the previous section, our longings for God are compared to hunger and thirst. And our enjoyment of God is compared to being satisfied with food and drink. If I have been hungry and now I am satisfied, what must have happened? I ate something! It turns out that eating is a great way to describe the transaction that takes place between a spiritually hungry person and the God who alone can satisfy him or her. Jesus capitalizes on this effective metaphor in one of his most famous sermons, "The Bread of Life Discourse," found in John 6. On the day before he preached this sermon, Jesus had fed the five thousand. Now the same crowd sought him out again; they were hungry and wanted him to provide them with another free meal. So he takes advantage of the context to teach them what is really worth living for and what is not. Jesus said, "I am the bread of life; whoever comes to me shall not hunger, and whoever believes in me shall never thirst" (v. 35). Jesus represents himself as bread—something we eat—and points out several ways he is different from literal bread and several ways he is like literal bread.

First, the differences: All physical bread eventually molds and goes bad, so Jesus says, "Do not work for the food that perishes, but for the food that endures to eternal life, which the Son of Man will give to you" (v. 27). Do not waste your life trying to satisfy the cravings of your immortal soul with food that will go bad and is therefore unsuitable for you. An animal meant to eat meat will not thrive on a diet of vegetables. A human made to feed on God will not thrive on a diet of earth. We were made to know God and enjoy him forever, and we cannot thrive on anything less than that. Again, even freshly baked physical bread can satisfy you only temporarily, but Jesus says, "I am the bread of life; whoever comes to me shall not hunger, and whoever believes in me shall never thirst" (v. 35). He offers us bread that can satisfy eternally. Nothing physical can ever make us deeply and permanently happy.

You were made to have fellowship with God. Jesus can restore this soul-satisfying fellowship. No matter how healthy your physical diet may be, you will eventually die. Jack LaLanne was one of the most famous fitness and nutrition gurus of the twentieth century. He stayed in shape and ate healthily until he died a very old man; but he did die. In contrast, Jesus describes himself as "the living bread that came down from heaven. If anyone eats of this bread, he will live forever" (v. 51).

Now for the similarities between Jesus and literal bread: When we eat bread, we take it into our bodies. It does us no good if we merely look at it. We must appropriate it by eating it. So we must appropriate Jesus into our lives. We must eat, or receive him, especially as a God-sent, crucified Savior: "Unless you eat the flesh of the Son of Man and drink his blood, you have no life in you" (v. 53). Further, similar to the way literal bread sustains our physical life, Jesus gives and sustains our spiritual life. "I am the living bread that came down from heaven. If anyone eats of this bread, he will live forever. And the bread that I will give for the life of the world is my flesh" (v. 51). Finally, when we eat bread it becomes part of our physical body. Similarly, Jesus says, "Whoever feeds on my flesh and drinks my blood abides in me, and I in him" (v. 56).

When we pray, "Give us this day our daily bread," we are asking God to continue to feed us and sustain us with the spiritual food he has provided in Christ.

Day 7

Bread is found in the Bible.

We know Christ and we feed on Christ based on what we read about him in the Bible. If you want to feed on Jesus, the Bread of Life, he is set on the table in the Bible. Come to the table and eat what God has prepared. Once I was a guest in a home where the woman of the house had spent all day preparing an abundant and delicious meal. A family with a little boy who would eat only crackers and peanut butter had also been invited to the feast. After all the platters and bowls of food had been passed and my plate was heaped up with the bounty of that table, the boy's plate was empty. He looked at his mother and smiled; she left the table and returned with a bag of peanut butter crackers, which he ate. How do you think the cook felt? What do you suppose God thinks about us when he has from eternity past been preparing Jesus, the Bread of Life, and we prefer our bag of peanut butter and crackers? I wrote earlier that before we are born again we are spiritually dead, and the main evidence of our deadness is that we fundamentally disagree with God about what is most important in life. Above all else, God prizes his Son. When we turn our nose up at Jesus, we are sure to incur his displeasure. God says, "This is my beloved Son. Listen to him. Feed on him." Yet we say, "We want our crackers!"

Our interaction with the Word of God ought to be similar to our interaction with food. To make this clear, the Holy Spirit, who inspired the Bible, sometimes uses food items to describe the truth: "Like newborn infants, long for the pure spiritual milk, that by it you may grow up into salvation—if indeed you have tasted that the Lord is good" (1 Peter 2:2–3). The rules of the Lord are "sweeter also than honey and drippings of the honeycomb" (Ps. 19:10).

Food can be beautiful to look at; it even looks good in art. I love old Dutch still-life paintings, and many of them depict food. It looks so good! Similarly, a skilled chef cares about how his culinary creations are presented. He puts it on a beautiful plate—maybe a zigzag of sauce drizzled artfully across the food, maybe a sprig of parsley for accent. But as beautiful as food can be to the eye, it is meant to be eaten. And so it is with the Word of God. It is meant to be taken in and chewed and savored and appropriated as nourishment to our spirits.

Some people staunchly defend the doctrine of the inerrancy of Scripture but apparently do not fill their hearts with the Bible, for they rarely talk about Bible truth. Many will say, "I believe the Bible is the word of God," but their practice reveals what they really think. Is it possible to genuinely believe that the Bible is the word of God and then rarely read it?

When we ask the Lord to give us this day our daily bread, we ought to be asking him for spiritual bread as well as physical and mental bread. But can we be sincere in our request if we then refuse to go to the cupboard where he keeps bread for his children? The Bible is a well-stocked storehouse of truth perfectly suited to satisfy our hungry hearts.

**FORGIVE US OUR DEBTS,
AS WE FORGIVE OUR DEBTORS**

THOUGHT #6

We agree with God
about sin and forgiveness.

Day 1

We want God to re-create us, and we agree to cooperate with our re-creation.

The Lord Jesus Christ is the only human being who has pleased God every moment of his existence. He never had a sinful thought or desire. He never did anything wrong. He "knew no sin" (2 Cor. 5:21). Beyond merely avoiding wrong, he always said and did what God wanted him to do. He always spoke the truth; he is "the faithful and true witness" (Rev. 3:14). Who but Jesus could honestly say, "I always do the things that are pleasing to him" (John 8:29)?

Jesus is the only human who has lived a perfect life, but he ought not to have been the only one. God originally created humans with the capacity to live sinless lives. There was the potential for everyone to say, "I always do the things that are pleasing to him." Can you imagine a world where everyone would have been as honest, thoughtful, and holy as Jesus? How happy we all would have been! It could have been our world, but Satan successfully tempted humans into rebelling against God, and our rebellion, or our *fall* into sin, has had far-reaching, devastating consequences. All humanity, by their fall, lost communion with God. We are no longer in harmony with his thoughts and ways. We think and act in ways that are contrary to his will, and often we do this deliberately. We refuse to cooperate with him, and sin itself is a refusal to cooperate with God.

Since God is an honest and just God, he kept his threat about what would happen if humans disobeyed him. He became angry with humans and put us under a dreadful curse. The curse made us liable to all miseries in this life, to death itself, and to the pains of hell forever.[1] Because he still requires humans to live a perfect life—after all, it is not his fault we became rebels—and no one is righteous, everyone is constantly accumulating a debt to God. We have a debt of righteousness we owe God, and we are unable to pay our debt. How different our sin-cursed world is from how

---

1 This phrase and connected ideas are found in the Baptist Catechism, Q. 22.

it began. When the first creation began, "the morning stars sang together and all the sons of God shouted for joy" (Job 38:7). Now our world is filled with the miserable, painful cries of billions of deeply indebted people estranged from our Creator.

With the coming of Christ, God commenced a new creation. The great goal of Christ's coming is to bring glory to God through re-creating humans so that we think and act like Jesus Christ. "For those whom he foreknew he also predestined to be conformed to the image of his Son, in order that he might be the firstborn among many brothers" (Rom. 8:29). You might think of Jesus as the eldest brother in the family, and God wants us to look like our older brother. So does Jesus; he said, "If anyone serves me, he must follow me" (John 12:26). The Bible says that Jesus has "called us to his own glory and excellence by which he has granted to us his precious and very great promises, so that through them you may become partakers of the divine nature, having escaped from the corruption that is in the world because of sinful desire" (2 Peter 1:3–4). God is creating a new world through the saving work of Christ, and Jesus is "the beginning of God's creation" (Rev. 3:14). Everyone who receives Christ is adopted into God's family and becomes a part of this new creation. "If anyone is in Christ, he is a new creation. The old has passed away; behold, the new has come" (2 Cor. 5:17). God is making a kingdom full of people who cherish Christ and do good works. "For we are his workmanship created in Christ Jesus for good works" (Eph. 2:10).

After his work on earth was done, Jesus returned to heaven, but he sent his Holy Spirit to continue this work of re-creating us to think and act like Jesus. "And we all, with unveiled face, beholding the glory of the Lord, are being transformed into the same image from one degree of glory to another. For this comes from the Lord who is the Spirit" (2 Cor. 3:18).

When a person becomes a follower of Jesus Christ, that person agrees that God needs to re-create him, and he agrees to cooperate with the process.

Day 2

We are sorry about our debt.

When we begin to agree with God about his new creation, and when we see that the goal of this new creation is to make us think and act like Jesus, we are confronted with a sober reality: we do not think and act like Jesus. If God expects us to look like Jesus, we are deeply in debt, and this debt is so enormous we will never be able to pay it. Our only hope is if God forgives us of the debt. God *will* forgive our debts, and it will be only because of his grace, but there are conditions.[2] One of these conditions is repentance.

God forgives the debt of those who repent. In the following section I explain more about repentance, but for now note that an essential element of repentance is that you are sorry for your debts to God. You know there is absolutely no point in telling God you are sorry about this debt if you do not even see the debt. Furthermore, you will not truly be sorry about it until you see that this debt is not someone else's fault; it is your fault. You must stop making excuses like, "Well, I'm only human," or "Nobody's perfect," trying to minimize your sin. Not only that, but you will only make matters worse if you say you are sorry about the debt when deep down you are thinking that it is "no big deal." You must agree with God that you owe him a debt you cannot pay and that it is a debt you have accumulated. You admit he has every right to be upset about it because you have failed to love him and glorify him, which is why he made humans in the first place, and this debt is a "big deal."

One more thing—you will only be insulting God should you say, "I am sorry about the debt," and you plan to keep on living the same sinful way, deliberately accumulating more and more debt. Sorry means *sad*. Are you really sad about something you fully intend to keep doing?

---

[2] "To escape the wrath and curse of God due to us for sin, God requireth of us faith in Jesus Christ, repentance unto life, with the diligent use of all the outward means whereby Christ communicateth to us the benefits of redemption" (The Baptist Catechism Q. 90).

Day 3

We agree with God about sin.

When Jesus commenced his public ministry on earth, his first teaching is summarized in one sentence: "Jesus came into Galilee, proclaiming the gospel of God, and saying, 'The time is fulfilled, and the kingdom of God is at hand; repent and believe in the gospel'" (Mark 1:14–15).

In the chapter on "Your Kingdom Come," I explained more fully what Jesus meant when he announced, "The kingdom of God is at hand," but using the language of this chapter, we might say that Jesus is declaring, "The time has come when God is going to reveal a new creation. The good news is that God is providing a way people in the new creation can have their debt to God forgiven. Do you want to have your debt forgiven and be part of God's new humanity? Then repent and believe the good news I am bringing."

What does it mean to repent? A simple definition is "to turn away from sin." This turning away from sin has several significant aspects to it. First, repentance unto life is a saving *grace*, and grace comes from God. You will not successfully repent without God's grace. So at the outset, ask God to help you to repent. Then, as outlined above, a repenting person must have a true sense of his sin—he sees the debt and is sorry for it. Further, no one ever truly repents unless he has some hope that God is a merciful God who will forgive anyone who repents and believes the gospel. "Whoever would draw near to God must believe that he exists and that he rewards those who seek him" (Heb. 11:6). True repentance cannot be separated from looking to God to give the mercy that he has provided in Christ. This mercy in Christ is called the gospel, and therefore Jesus says, "Repent and believe the gospel."

What Jesus has done to make forgiveness possible is explained fully in the New Testament, but one small book in the New Testament was written "so that you may believe that Jesus is the Christ, the Son of God, and that by believing you may have life in his name" (John 20:31). That small book is the Gospel of John, and the average reader can read the entire book in well under three hours. I encourage you to read it.

Many years ago, I was teaching freshman composition at a secular university to about thirty students. When it was time for me to teach them how to do a book review, a common part of freshman composition classes, I told them, "Rather than have each of you read a book of your own choosing, I am going to assign everyone to read the same book. You will be pleased to know that it is only a small book. It is the Gospel of John found in the Bible. Can everyone get access to a Bible?" You might be thinking, *Can you do that in a secular university?* Well, you can do it once! When the students turned in their book reviews on the Gospel of John, two students wrote something like, "I never knew anything about Christianity, but after reading this book, I want to be a Christian."

When you repent, then, you must have a true sense of your sin and some hope that God will show you mercy through Christ. When God reveals these truths to you, you will be sorry for your sin, and you will hate it. You must turn from your sin and turn to God with the full intention of obeying God for the rest of your life.[3]

When we pray, "Forgive us our debts," we are agreeing with God about sin.

DAY 4

We need God's forgiveness.

When we pray, "Forgive us our debts," we show that we agree with God about sin: it is a debt. We also show that we agree with God about how this debt must be resolved: we want him to forgive us.

---

[3] This information about repentance is based on the answer to question 92 in the Baptist Catechism: "Repentance unto life is a saving grace, whereby a sinner, out of a true sense of his sin, and apprehension of the mercy of God in Christ, doth, with grief and hatred of his sin, turn from it unto God, with full purpose of and endeavor after new obedience."

When you forgive someone of a debt, you no longer expect the debtor to pay what he owes. This is what we are asking God to do for us. Why would he do such a thing?

First, God is very merciful, and he delights to show mercy. "Who is a God like you, pardoning iniquity and passing over transgression for the remnant of his inheritance? He does not retain his anger forever, because he delights in steadfast love" (Mic. 7:18). God once described himself as "The Lord, the Lord, a God merciful and gracious, slow to anger, and abounding in steadfast love and faithfulness, keeping steadfast love for thousands, forgiving iniquity and transgression and sin, but who will by no means clear the guilty, visiting the iniquity of the fathers on the children and the children's children, to the third and the fourth generation" (Ex. 34:6–7). In this description of himself, God lists nine qualities about his character, and seven of them point to his predisposition to be merciful!

What about those other two qualities? They sound pretty frightening—he will not clear the guilty, and he visits iniquity. These two qualities reveal that he does not show his mercy indiscriminately but in a particular way. He will bestow mercy on those whose debt of guilt and iniquity has been paid for. God's mercy does not nullify his justice. He forgives sins because those sins have been paid for by Jesus. "We implore you on behalf of Christ, be reconciled to God. For our sake he made him to be sin who knew no sin, so that in him we might become the righteousness of God" (2 Cor. 5:20–21). "He was pierced for our transgressions; he was crushed for our iniquities; upon him was the chastisement that brought us peace, and with his wounds we are healed. All we like sheep have gone astray; we have turned—every one—to his own way; and the Lord has laid on him the iniquity of us all" (Isa. 53:5–6). God is merciful, and he bestows his mercy on sinners and forgives us our debts because he is satisfied with the payment Jesus made on our behalf.

When we pray, "Forgive us our debts," we are acknowledging that God is a merciful God, Jesus is a merciful Savior, and that the only way we can be right with God is if he forgives us our debts because of Jesus.

Day 5

We show we have been forgiven when we forgive others.

Asking for forgiveness through Christ is a good indication that God has begun to correct our thinking about the essential issues of life—we agree with him about our debt and about his Son. Just as significant, God is teaching us to think like him as we relate to people. In particular, God wants us to have a perspective that makes us eager and willing to forgive people who have sinned against us. We pray, "Forgive us our debts, as we also have forgiven our debtors" (Matt. 6:12).

After teaching his disciples the Model Prayer, Jesus immediately gives further explanation of this petition. He says, "For if you forgive others their trespasses, your heavenly Father will also forgive you, but if you do not forgive others their trespasses, neither will your Father forgive your trespasses" (vv. 14–15). This does not mean we earn God's forgiveness through forgiving others, but it does mean that a person who has been forgiven by God will forgive others. If you cannot forgive, you have not been forgiven.

Earlier we learned that when you forgive someone of a debt, you no longer expect the debtor to pay what he owes. Must the debtor repent before you forgive him? Yes and no. Yes because real forgiveness is inseparable from reconciliation. There must be an intention of repairing the relationship that was interrupted by the debt, and both the forgiver and the forgiven must have this intention to repair. God himself does not forgive those who do not repent. So, must the debtor repent first? Yes. But the answer is also no, and God sets for us the example of what forgiveness looks like when the debtor has not yet repented. God is ready to forgive those who repent. This readiness is not full-grown forgiveness, but it is forgiveness in the seed.

I believe this "seed forgiveness" is what Jesus must be describing in Mark 11:25 when he says, "And whenever you stand praying, forgive, if you have anything against anyone, so that your Father also who is in heaven may forgive you your trespasses." In the scenario that Jesus describes, there is no time for going to the person to try to work things out. That seems like it must be the logical next step, but at the moment you are praying, Jesus says, plant the seed of forgiveness in your heart. When someone sins against us, or incurs a debt to us, we must not only be ready to forgive but also be eager for it to happen. Readiness to forgive means that we are not nursing a grudge. We are not hoping something bad happens to the person. In fact, we pray for them. We seek God's blessing on them: "Bless those who persecute you; bless and do not curse them" (Rom. 12:14). And if they repent and ask for our forgiveness, we give it freely and joyfully. After all, that is how God treated us. And our sin against God is so much greater than any sin that someone might commit against us.

How can we forgive? Sometimes people have been so viciously bad to us. Forgive them because you want to please Jesus. Forgive through the power of the Spirit of Christ who dwells in you. "Let all bitterness and wrath and anger and clamor and slander be put away from you, along with all malice. Be kind to one another, tenderhearted, forgiving one another, as God in Christ forgave you" (Eph. 4:31–32).

DAY 6

We see our own indebtedness to God as we strive to forgive others.

When praying, "Forgive us our debts," it may be that an earnest and sincere lover of God has trouble remembering any particular debts. They are not so arrogant as to presume sinlessness, but no particular sins spring to mind. A good way to discover the sins that may be hiding from us (or that we do not want to find) is to think about the second part of the petition: "as we forgive our debtors." When you think of people you need to forgive, what have they done that needs forgiveness?

Reflect on the most recent occurrence of your being irritated with someone, or perhaps think of a person who consistently irritates you. Why are you irritated with the person? Almost without fail we are irritated because they did not behave toward us as we thought he or she ought to have behaved. We had a right to expect something from that person, and they had an obligation, or debt, to pay it. What is my perspective toward those disappointed expectations? Was I pure and righteous in my expectations? Was I patient and submissive to God in my disappointment? Did I treat the offender—the debtor—with the respect due to a human created in the image of God?

If God were to answer my prayer exactly as I ask him in this petition, "Forgive me *as* I forgive my debtors," would I be completely forgiven? A holy hermit might emerge from such a session of self-examination thinking himself to be blameless, but there are few who live in society who can examine themselves under this spotlight and come away saying, "I have nothing to confess."

Furthermore, the sorts of sins others commit against us that we feel most keenly are usually the same sorts of sins we commit against our Father in heaven. Do I feel that my wife has slighted me? Perhaps she failed to notice something I did for her benefit. How often I have neglected to thank God for his flood of blessings in my life. Has an employer failed to fairly compensate me for my labor? I have failed to give the Lord the glory due his name. Did my friend ignore me when I was talking? How often I turn a deaf ear to the Lord. So, the very phrasing of this petition causes a searchlight to focus on my own heart, and through examining my disappointed expectations, I see my own failings in my relationship with the Lord.

Day 7

We have a debt of love to God.

Debt is an obligation to pay something. Once a financial debt is paid, the one-time debtor no longer needs to plead with the creditor for clemency, and the creditor stops sending notifications for the amount due. So, if Jesus paid our debt on the cross, why are we taught to ask daily for God to forgive us our debts?

Jesus paid for us the debt that was due to God, the righteous judge, and in so doing, he transferred us from the prison for debtors to the house of the Father, and now we are part of God's family. In an earthly family there are debts of family obligation. There are attitudes of respect and reverence that are due to the father and mother. There are responsibilities that parents have to children, that siblings have to one another, and so on. And that is how it is in God's family. We have debts of obligation that keep peace and fellowship in our familial relationships, especially with our Father. When we become aware of these unfulfilled debts, we ask our Father to forgive us, not because we fear damnation but because we value peace with him.

AND LEAD US NOT INTO TEMPTATION, BUT DELIVER US FROM EVIL

THOUGHT #7

God is in control of all persons
and all circumstances.

DAY 1

Temptation is a test.

In May of 1976, my dad and I were sitting in Buckeye Stadium in Columbus, Ohio, watching the Ohio High School state track meet. I had finished competing in the high-jump competition earlier that day (I did not win), and now we could relax and watch some of the best high-school athletes in the world. We were especially eager to see the 440-yard dash (now the 400-meters) because the race would feature the two athletes who had run the two fastest times in the United States that season. Number One and Number Two would be going head-to-head in the state meet! Even the legendary Jesse Owens had come to watch. The race was every bit as exciting as we had anticipated. When the starting gun sounded, Number One exploded out of the blocks and set a blazingly fast pace. Number Two was right behind him. Dad and I were sitting about fifty yards from the finish line, and when the two runners were right in front of us, Number Two passed Number One. Then something happened that made the entire crowd gasp in shocked disbelief: Number One pushed Number Two in the back and both runners fell. In a flash, both runners regained their feet and finished the race well ahead of the field. Number Two finished in first place that day, and amazingly, he set a new state record despite the fall.

The push and the fall occurred so quickly that it was hard to tell what had happened. There was no instant replay. Did Number One push Number Two on purpose, attempting to cheat? Or had he merely stumbled at the exact moment Number Two was passing him and accidentally fall into his opponent? You can get disqualified either way, but we wanted to know: Did he do it on purpose? If he did, then his intention was clear—he was trying to cheat. We admire the drive to win, but we know there are rules on how to win fairly, and a good sport wants to compete according to the rules.

Temptation is a test. When Satan is doing the tempting, his intention is to get us to win by cheating. When God is doing the tempting, his intention is to train us to win fairly.

Does God tempt? If you are familiar with the Bible, you may be aware of a verse in the book of James that says this: "Let no one say when he is tempted, 'I am being tempted by God,' for God cannot be tempted with evil, and he himself tempts no one. But each person is tempted when he is lured and enticed by his own desire" (1:13–14). On the other hand, there are several places in the Bible where God is said to tempt. He tempted Abraham (Gen. 22:1), he tempted Israel at Marah (Ex. 15:25), and he left some of the nations in Canaan to tempt Israel (Judg. 3:1–4). If you take the time to look up the Scriptures referenced in the previous sentence, you may find that your translation says that God *tested* Abraham and Israel rather than that God *tempted* them. In fact, in the Greek translation of the Old Testament, which is the version most often quoted by Jesus and the apostles, the Greek word used to say that God tempted/tested Abraham and Israel is the same word James uses when he says that God "tempts no one." That's right: the exact same Greek word can be used in some contexts to mean *tempt*, and in other contexts it means *test*. Both tempting and testing entail a trial. Whether the trial is a temptation or a test depends on who is orchestrating the trial and what his ultimate purpose is. I had a basketball coach who would make us run sprints to punish us and make us suffer. I had other coaches who would make us run sprints to train us and make us better. Satan uses trials to produce rebellion in us. God uses trials to produce godliness in us. I think the context of the entire Bible leads us to understand James 1:13 to say, "God cannot be tempted with evil, and he himself tempts no one *to produce evil.*"

Day 2

We honor God when we pass his tests or when we learn from our failures.

Temptation is a test. For that matter, everything that happens to us in life is a test. Poverty is a test; so is prosperity. Sickness is a test, but so also is health. Losing is a test, and winning is a test. Persecution and popularity are both tests. "The crucible is for silver, and the furnace is for gold, and a man is tested by his praise" (Prov. 27:21).

When we take tests in school, we either pass or fail. If we pass, we may pass only barely, or we may pass with excellence. If we fail, we may fail badly, or we may be just short of a passing grade. Sometimes failing serves a good purpose because it shows us where our weaknesses are. I have had more than one student thank me for giving them a failing grade because it startled them out of their laziness and set them on the path of successful diligence.

Passing a test well does us good and brings honor to our Father. My older sister was three years ahead of me in school. She earned a good reputation as an intelligent, diligent student, and she brought honor to our family by the way she behaved at school. Then I came along. I did not like school. Prior to my conversion at age fourteen, I was not a diligent student. The teachers who had taught my sister must have asked, "What is wrong with this boy? His sister was so different. We thought he came from a well-disciplined family, but he is not acting like it. The fact that he has the potential to do better makes his poor performance all the more inexcusable."

We do not want to bring dishonor to our Father in heaven. Even when we are pursuing him with all our heart, we feel our frailty and our sinfulness. We are so easily distracted from what is most precious. We know we are liable to fail the tests we may face that day, so we pray, "Lead us not into temptation, but deliver us from evil." We are asking God to exercise his sovereign control over the people and circumstances of our lives so we do not fail him and dishonor him. We want to be able to say, "I have learned in whatever situation I am to be content. I know how to be brought low, and I know how to abound. In any and every circumstance, I have learned the secret of facing plenty and hunger, abundance and need. I can do all things through him who strengthens me" (Phil. 4:11–13). Paul said that he had learned the secret. That secret is making our happiness consist in having and knowing God to be our God, and saying, "Whom have I in heaven but you? And there is nothing on earth that I desire besides you. My flesh and my heart may fail, but God is the strength of my heart and my portion forever" (Ps. 73:25–26). We will be unshakably and eternally happy when we can truly say, "The LORD is my chosen portion and my cup; you hold my lot. The lines have fallen for me in pleasant places; indeed, I have a beautiful inheritance" (Ps. 16:5–6).

DAY 3

When God tests us, he intends to do us good.

As noted earlier, the Greek word translated *temptation* in the Lord's Prayer is a word used to describe what Satan does but also to describe what God does. When Satan tempts, he is using his powers and resources to attempt to get us to sin and dishonor God by rebelling against God. When God tempts, or tests, he is using his powers and resources to get us to choose wisely and honor him by trusting him.

For nearly thirty years I have made and used self-bows. A self-bow is a bow made from all-natural materials, and as the name implies, I make it my*self*. The real skill of making a good self-bow is in the tillering, which is the process of getting a stick of wood to bend evenly without breaking. Tillering is a fairly simple process: you remove wood where the future bow is not bending enough, and you leave the wood alone where it is bending too much. It takes a long time to do it right, and if you get in too much of a hurry, you will end up with either a children's bow or worse, a very labor-intensive piece of firewood. As soon as the piece of wood will bend enough to put a string on it, you begin to pull it back just a little bit, and you look at it to make sure it is bending evenly. If it is not, you take the string off and fix the problem. After attempting to fix the problem, you put the string back on it, and pull it a little farther. This process is repeated again and again, testing it over and over, until it is bending evenly at your target weight and draw length. It is a proud (and anxious) moment when you knock an arrow on the string and shoot it and the bow does not break. It gives one a real sense of accomplishment to show someone the bow and say, "I made that."

In all those tests I perform on the wood I am forming into a bow, I am not trying to break the bow. I am trying to keep it from breaking; I am trying to perfect the bow. I am getting rid of the excess material that is keeping the wood from becoming a functional, beautiful bow. All the testing is essential to the finished product. I test the bow so that its flaws will be revealed and I can fix them. This is the way God tests us. His goal is not to break us; his goal is to fashion us into a person who is useful to him and who glorifies him. He tests us to reveal what is getting in the way of our becoming more like Jesus. When he is finished with us, he will be able to say of us, "I made that," and it will be to the praise of his glory. When we pray, "Lead us not into temptation," we are asking the Lord not to bend us past the breaking point. In his presence we are reminding him and ourselves, "No temptation has overtaken you that is not common to man. God is faithful, and he will not let you be tempted beyond your ability, but with the temptation he will also provide the way of escape, that you may be able to endure it" (1 Cor. 10:13).

Day 4

Satan's temptations are illegitimate shortcuts to a legitimate goal.

When Satan tempts us, he tries to lure us into taking an illegitimate shortcut to a legitimate goal. He is trying to get us to get something good by cheating. Winning the race is a noble goal. Winning the race by pushing down your opponent is an illegitimate shortcut.

Almost every temptation from Satan comes with the promise that we will be able to enjoy some pleasure without going through all the steps that God requires. The promised pleasure is nearly always something God has created and allows us to enjoy under the right conditions. The legitimate, God-given pleasure decays into a sinful pleasure when we love it too much or when we love it too little or when we try to enjoy it in a way that God never intended. It is legitimate to own a bicycle; it is an illegitimate shortcut to steal it. It is legitimate to enjoy the pleasures of physical intimacy; it is illegitimate to enjoy them outside the context of a monogamous, heterosexual marriage. God created all the wholesome pleasures, and Satan has never created one. So Satan tempts us by presenting us with shortcuts to enjoying the pleasures that God has reserved for those who seek them the right way.

Paradise Lost is a brilliant, book-length poem that explores how sin entered the world through Adam's succumbing to Satan's temptation and disobeying God. That is how paradise was lost. Some years after John Milton had written *Paradise Lost*, he wrote something like a sequel called *Paradise Regained*. I had enjoyed *Paradise Lost*, and so I decided to read *Paradise Regained*. I assumed that it would be about the work Christ did on the cross and how he regained paradise for us by his death, burial, and resurrection. To my surprise, *Paradise Regained* was entirely about Christ's temptation in the wilderness. As I pondered this, it dawned on me: Paradise was lost because the first representative man, Adam, succumbed to temptation. Paradise is regained because the last representative man, Jesus Christ, successfully resisted temptation.

You can read about Christ's temptation in the wilderness in Matthew 4, Mark 1, and Luke 4. What you will find there is that the goals with which Satan tempts the Lord are all legitimate goals. It was legitimate for Jesus to want to satisfy his hunger, but it would have been illegitimate for him to misuse his miraculous power in a way that God never commanded. It was legitimate for Christ to gain the admiration of the people of Jerusalem, but it would have been illegitimate for him to do it by showing off and tempting God by throwing himself from the pinnacle of the temple. Again, it was legitimate for Christ to possess the kingdoms of the world but illegitimate for him to gain possession through worshiping Satan. Jesus saw the shortcuts as the sinful alternatives that they were. He rebuffed Satan, he did things God's way, and in maintaining his perfect innocence, he became fully qualified to be the one to regain paradise for his children. "Although he was a son, he learned obedience through what he suffered. And being made perfect, he became the source of eternal salvation to all who obey him" (Heb. 5:8–9). Now Satan has been defeated, Jesus has received all authority, and John the Revelator heard "loud voices in heaven, saying, 'The kingdom of the world has become the kingdom of our Lord and of his Christ, and he shall reign forever and ever'" (Rev. 11:15).

Day 5

Our sinful hearts make us vulnerable to temptation.

The Bible says that Jesus "in every respect has been tempted as we are, yet without sin" (Heb. 4:15). If Jesus was tempted as we are, did he want to sin? The answer is no. So far, in our consideration of temptation we have focused primarily on the intention of the person doing the tempting: God's benevolent intention, and Satan's malevolent intention. Now we turn to consider the state of the heart of the person being tempted.

When Satan tempted Christ, Satan was trying to find some weakness or vulnerability in him. He never found it. Throughout history, from the garden of Eden on, Satan had always been able to find some weakness in every human he tempted. There was always a chink in the armor of defense. He got Moses to speak and act in anger. He got David to lust. He got Elijah to despair. In every human, Satan found a sinful fallen nature with a propensity to listen to his lies and take the shortcuts he offered. But not in Jesus. Satan offered the shortcuts to Jesus, but the Lord always saw them for what they were: sinful departures from God's perfect will. You will never see a dove sitting beside a vulture feeding on a dead carcass. It is not the dove's nature to eat such stuff. He will die of starvation rather than feed on carrion. And so it was with our Lord. He never wanted to sin; it was not in his nature. On the evening he was betrayed, Jesus told his disciples, "I will no longer talk much with you, for the ruler of this world is coming. He has no claim on me [literally, *he has nothing in me*], but I do as the Father has commanded me, so that the world may know that I love the Father" (John 14:30–31). Satan, with all his wolves, was fast approaching, but just as he had found Jesus invulnerable at the beginning of the Lord's public ministry, he still, at the end of Christ's ministry, had nothing in Jesus to take advantage of or to lay claim to.

Even after our conversion, sinfulness remains in our nature, and that makes us susceptible to temptation in a way that Jesus was not. In our sinfulness, sometimes we want to take the shortcut. When you build a fire, you start by lighting tinder—small, extremely flammable material that catches fire easily. If you just barely touch a lighted match to dry pine needles, they immediately catch fire. Our sinful hearts are like those dry pine needles. The lighted match of temptation can inflame our desires and lead us into sin. It is not God's fault. Again, "let no one say when he is tempted, 'I am being tempted by God,' for God cannot be tempted with evil, and he himself tempts no one. But each person is tempted when he is lured and enticed by his own desire. Then desire when it has conceived gives birth to sin, and sin when it is fully grown brings forth death" (James 1:13–15). As we have seen already and will see still further, God does tempt or test people, but he cannot be tempted with evil, and his goal in tempting is not ultimately the production of evil; rather, his goal is the accomplishment of his eternal purpose, which is good. The primary teaching of this passage from James is that we cannot blame God for our sin. Our hearts are sinful, we feel our vulnerability, and so "we pray that God would either keep us from being tempted to sin or support and deliver us when we are tempted."[1]

DAY 6

"Note then the kindness and the severity of God" (Rom. 11:22).

Anyone who reads and believes the Bible ought to know that God may do anything he pleases, but many are reluctant to embrace the truth that God actually does all that he pleases. God is in absolute control of all persons and all circumstances. He "works all things according to the counsel of his will" (Eph. 1:11). "He does according to his will among the host of heaven and among the inhabitants of the earth; and none can stay his hand or say to him, 'What have you done?'" (Dan. 4:35). "Our God is in the heavens; he does all that he pleases" (Ps. 115:3).

This is very comforting. Because he controls all things, he makes "all things work together for good, for those who are called according to his purpose" (Rom. 8:28). He is able to thwart the attacks evil persons attempt against his people so that "no weapon that is fashioned against you shall succeed" (Isa. 54:17). The wicked may try to curse God's people, but "instead the LORD your God turned the curse into a blessing for you, because the LORD

---

1 The Baptist Catechism, Q. 113.

your God loved you" (Deut. 23:5). Joseph was able to say to his brothers, "You meant evil against me, but God meant it for good" (Gen. 50:20). Ultimately, nothing bad can happen to one of God's children. We must learn that every unpleasant situation we face is either for our correction or for our training. "It is for discipline that you have to endure. God is treating you as sons. For what son is there whom his father does not discipline? If you are left without discipline, in which all have participated, then you are illegitimate children and not sons" (Heb. 12:7–8). The glorified Jesus says, "Those whom I love, I reprove and discipline, so be zealous and repent" (Rev. 3:19).

But, O Lord, lead us not into temptation! God leads us into temptation when he lets us feel the natural consequences of our sin. I know a man who used to raise silver foxes for their fur. The foxes were vicious and would bite anything inserted through the wire of their cages. When it was time to kill the foxes, the man would put an electric probe into the cage, and the foxes would bite the probe and immediately die from the surge of electricity. Their vicious nature led them to their own destruction. God, do not let me suffer the just consequences of my vicious, sinful heart. Do not give me up to the lusts of my heart (Rom. 1:24). Do not give me up to my stubborn heart to follow my own counsel (Ps. 81:12). May it not be said of us, "He gave them their request, but sent leanness into their soul" (Ps. 106:15 KJV). Do not let me live my life for nothing. "Behold, is it not from the LORD of hosts that peoples labor merely for fire, and nations weary themselves for nothing?" (Hab. 2:13). Lead us not into temptation, but deliver us from our own evil desires.

God leads us into temptation when he lets evil men have their way with us. "For you, O God, have tested us; you have tried us as silver is tried. You brought us into the net; you laid a crushing burden on our backs; you let men ride over our heads; we went through fire and through water" (Ps. 66:10–12). "He turned their hearts to hate his people, to deal craftily with his servants" (Ps. 105:25). Lead us not into temptation, but deliver us from evil men.

God leads us into temptation when he withholds gracious, softening influences. Modeling clay naturally gets hard if you leave it out of a protective container. My heart will grow hard if God leaves me to myself. One of the most chilling sentences in the Bible is this: "Ephraim is joined to idols; leave him alone" (Hos. 4:17). After he had delivered some unpopular teaching, Jesus's "disciples came and said to him, 'Do you know that the Pharisees were offended when they heard this saying?' He answered, 'Every plant that my heavenly Father has not planted will be rooted up. Let them alone; they are blind guides'" (Matt. 15:12–14). Oh, Father, do not ever say of me, "Let him alone." Lead us not into temptation, but deliver us from deluded self-rule.

God leads us into temptation when he allows evil spirits access to us, as he did to Adam and Eve (Genesis 3) and as he did to Job (Job 1, 2). How well Peter knew the truth of what he wrote: "Your adversary the devil prowls around like a roaring lion, seeking someone to devour" (1 Peter 5:8). Lord Jesus, pray for me like you did for Peter: "Simon, Simon, behold, Satan demanded to have you, that he might sift you like wheat, but I have prayed for you that your faith may not fail" (Luke 22:31–32). Lead us not into temptation, but deliver us from the Evil One.

DAY 7

"Behold, as the eyes of servants look to the hand of their master, as the eyes of a maidservant to the hand of her mistress, so our eyes look to the LORD our God, till he has mercy upon us" (Ps. 123:2).

God's leading us into the kind of temptations just described is not his first choice of how to lead us and shape us. Allow a right-handed man to say that God blesses with his right hand but disciplines with his left. "He takes the rod with reluctance, and he lays it aside with pleasure."[2] He says, "I will instruct you and teach you

---

2 Jay, *Morning Exercises*, 352.

in the way you should go; I will counsel you with my eye upon you. Be not like a horse or a mule, without understanding, which must be curbed with bit and bridle, or it will not stay near you" (Ps. 32:8–9). To control a horse or a mule, we put a bit into its mouth, which enables us to control the animal as the bit exerts pressure to the sensitive spot of its mouth if it resists our directions with the reins. God says to his children, "I can control you that way when necessary, and I will do it rather than let you perish in your sin, but there is a better way: I will guide you with my eye." Perhaps you remember the way your mother or father could correct you with a disapproving look or encourage you with an approving look. But if the look didn't work, then something more severe was likely to follow. "Do you presume on the riches of his kindness and forbearance and patience, not knowing that God's kindness is meant to lead you to repentance?" (Rom. 2:4). Let us learn what we ought to learn from God's eye and render it unnecessary for God to pick up his rod.

But should it be necessary for God to pick up his rod, we pray that he show himself to be a God who "does not deal with us according to our sins, nor repay us according to our iniquities. For as high as the heavens are above the earth, so great is his steadfast love toward those who fear him; as far as the east is from the west, so far does he remove our transgressions from us. As a father shows compassion to his children, so the LORD shows compassion to those who fear him. For he knows our frame; he remembers that we are dust" (Ps. 103:10–14). When David had sinned and God gave him a choice of punishments, David said, "I am in great distress. Let us fall into the hand of the LORD, for his mercy is great; but let me not fall into the hand of man" (2 Sam. 24:14). In praying, "lead us not into temptation, but deliver us from evil," we are asking something similar: "Father, you are a kind and gracious God. If it is necessary to discipline me, please let me fall into your hand, and deliver me from the Evil One and from the evil of my own sinful, unbelieving heart."

Part III

Praying in Jesus's Name

If you have the Lord's Prayer memorized, then you probably know that in the King James Version of the Bible, the prayer concludes with the statement, "Thine is the kingdom, and the power, and the glory, for ever. Amen" (Matt. 6:13). This concluding statement is found in some ancient manuscripts but not in others, so conservative, Bible-believing scholars disagree as to whether it was part of the original manuscript of Matthew's Gospel. I am not enough of a scholar to weigh in on this discussion, but it would certainly be appropriate if we want to conclude our praying by ascribing kingdom, power, and glory to God. It is quite similar to something in one of David's prayers in which he said, "Thine, O Lord is the greatness, and the power, and the glory, and the victory, and the majesty: for all that is in the heaven and in the earth is thine; thine is the kingdom, O Lord, and thou art exalted as head above all" (1 Chron. 29:11 KJV). As noted in the Baptist Catechism, this conclusion "teacheth us to take our encouragement in prayer from God only, and in our prayers to praise him" (Q. 114).

It Does Not Mean This

I rarely hear anyone conclude his or her prayer by saying, "Thine is the kingdom, and the power, and the glory forever. Amen." Nearly everyone who prays in public, whether in church or before a meal, concludes his prayer by saying, "In Jesus's name we pray. Amen." I suspect few Christians give much thought to what it means to say, "In Jesus's name I pray," and I fear that, consequently, it has just become the standard way of saying, "My prayer is now concluded." When I was a boy, that is certainly what I thought it meant, because it would confuse me when someone used the phrase in the middle of his prayer. I thought it was time to open my eyes and look around. It was almost as misleading to me as when a long-winded preacher said, "Finally," and then went on to preach for another fifteen minutes. I figured you were supposed to quit when you said, "In Jesus's name I pray." However, it is not a fancy way to say, "I'm done."

I have also heard some well-meaning folks assert that saying "In Jesus's name I pray" is a sure indicator that someone is a Christian and anyone who does not say it is probably an imposter. They may be right, but not necessarily. I admit that I do worry about the spiritual state of professing Christians who agree not to mention the name of Jesus in public prayers lest it offend nonbelievers or practitioners of other religions. Under the auspices of avoiding sectarianism, they come awfully close to being ashamed of Jesus before men, which will definitely come back to bite them. We cannot come into God's presence and expect our prayers to be heard unless we do pray in Jesus's name, but simply saying the phrase does not guarantee we are in fact coming in Jesus's name.

Some Christians seem to think that the phrase "In Jesus's name I pray" is something like a magic incantation that must be said just exactly right or God will not hear your prayer. My dad told me that when he was a little boy, if after saying his prayers at night, he climbed into bed and realized he had forgotten to conclude his prayer by saying "In Jesus's name I pray," he figured his whole prayer was disqualified, and he had to get out of bed and start his prayer all over again.

So, what does it mean for us to pray in Jesus's name? At least these three things: We are coming to God through Christ, we are coming to God like Christ, and we are coming to God for Christ.

We Are Coming to God through Christ

On the night he was betrayed, Jesus told his disciples, "Whatever you ask of the Father in my name, he will give it to you. Until now you have asked nothing in my name. Ask, and you will receive, that your joy may be full" (John 16:23–24). Note that he said to them, "Until now you have asked nothing in my name." Certainly his disciples were already converted men and had been praying to God as all converted persons do. If they had not been praying in Jesus's name, how had they been praying? They had been praying as old covenant believers. Perhaps they had been thinking of God primarily as the God of Abraham, Isaac, and Jacob, and that was an appropriate way for them to think, and they offered their prayer accordingly. Perhaps they had been praying to God as the God who delivered Israel out of Egyptian bondage or the God who gave the law to Moses, and again, these were appropriate ways for them to approach God. But Jesus was about to finish the work that qualified him to be "the guarantor of a better covenant" (Heb. 7:22), and the old covenant was about to become obsolete. "In speaking of a new covenant, he makes the first one obsolete" (Heb. 8:13), and "he does away with the first in order to establish the second" (Heb. 10:9). From that time on, his disciples are to approach God "by the new and living way that he opened for us through the curtain, that is, through his flesh" (Heb. 10:20). Praying in Jesus's name means that we now pray to God as new covenant believers.

Only born-again Christians can pray in Jesus's name. God has revealed that the only way we may approach him is through Jesus. "And there is salvation in no one else, for there is no other name under heaven given among men by which we must be saved" (Acts 4:12). Jesus himself said, "I am the way, and the truth, and the life. No one comes to the Father except through me" (John 14:6). He also said, "Whoever does not honor the Son does not honor the Father who sent him" (John 5:23). No matter how sincere, how devout, or how upright a person might be, if he is not honoring Jesus, he is not honoring God. When we attempt to pray to God while ignoring or rejecting Jesus's teaching, commands, and his work of redemption, God is not pleased. No wonder. If you want to make a loving parent angry, just disrespect her child. Can you imagine saying to the mother of a soldier who had given his life for his country, "I do not think your son is worthy to be honored, but would you do me a favor?" God sent his Son to be our Savior. God poured out his wrath on Jesus when he bled on the cross. God authenticated Christ's work and honored him by raising him from the dead and seating him at his own right hand where he gave him all power and authority. After having done all that, ought he listen to the prayers of people who disrespect his Son, treat his Son's dying work like it is worthless, and act as if they ought to get favors from him anyway? It is an insult to reject God's offer of grace through Christ and then say, "But God, there's no need for us to be narrow-minded. It is true that I do not believe in your Son, but could you do a few things for me?" Apart from Christ, you have no reason to think that God will answer your prayers. A person who prays without faith "must not suppose that he will receive anything from the Lord" (James 1:7). God will not be pleased with your prayers, for "without faith it is impossible to please him" (Heb. 11:6). In fact, your prayers will even be obnoxious to him: "If one turns away his ear from hearing the law, even his prayer is an abomination" (Prov. 28:9).

Perhaps it seems narrow-minded or even bigoted to say that God does not hear the prayers of people who are not coming to him through Christ. Remember that I am not the one who said it. Jesus said it. When he said it, he was speaking the truth. We are not doing well if in the interest of being friendly or open-minded we disagree with God's own messenger and pretend that people can gain God's favor some way other than through Jesus, who is the way.

We Are Coming to God like Christ

Prayer is more than merely asking God for favors or thanking him for blessings or even acknowledging his greatness and worshiping him. Fundamentally, prayer is thinking like Jesus in God's presence. As I maintain in the first chapter, prayer is a tool to remake us to think like Jesus, but to take it a step further, it is also true that the reason we have been remade to think like Jesus is so we might pray like Jesus. Prayer is more than a tool of sanctification; prayer is the goal of sanctification. Prayer is both means and goal. This "thinking like Jesus in God's presence" is essentially what it means to pray in Jesus's name, and this makes it even more obvious that it is impossible for anyone even to begin to do this until he or she becomes a devoted follower of Jesus.

A Brief Digression

In light of this, a couple questions arise. Ought we teach our unconverted children to pray? And ought we to encourage unbelievers to pray? The answer to both questions is yes. All people are responsible to pray, whether God is disposed to hear them or not. And to be fair, it is not simply that God does not hear the prayers of nonbelievers; nonbelievers do not truly pray. They may say prayer-like words, and they may address these words to whatever being they conceive God to be, and they may say them earnestly and devoutly, but they are not thinking like Jesus in the presence of the God and Father of our Lord Jesus Christ. If God is not listening to you when you pray, you are really just talking into the air. You are like a child talking into a play telephone—there is no one on the other end. You are having a pretend conversation. It is not prayer.

If a person wants to stop pretending to pray and truly pray, the first step is to repent of sin and receive Christ as Savior and Lord. When people are not right with God, they do not really want to pray and, therefore, they cannot pray. Their inability is a result of their disobedience, so it is not God's fault that rebels cannot pray. Yet all humans are responsible to do what God requires, and God requires everyone to pray. We may suppress the truth, but that does not make the truth disappear, nor does it make the penalty for suppressing truth disappear. "For the wrath of God is revealed from heaven against all ungodliness and unrighteousness of men, who by their unrighteousness suppress the truth" (Rom. 1:18). One reason for his wrath is that "although they knew God, they did not honor him as God or give thanks to him" (v. 21). In other words, his wrath comes because people do not pray. God does not suspend his righteous requirements because sinful humans have rendered themselves incapable of obedience.

So, yes, we ought to teach our unconverted children to pray, and we ought to urge non-Christians to pray because God requires it. It is his law. Any earnest attempt to pray may convince them of how unfit they are to pray. God uses his law is to show us our sinful inability and to drive us to seek salvation through receiving Christ. What should an unconverted person pray? "God be merciful to me, a sinner." "God, please save me." "God, please grant me repentance and faith." "God, have mercy on me for Jesus's sake." "Lord, you have said that you would save sinners; please save me."

Back to the Point

Praying like Jesus requires some conscious effort. Earlier in this book I wrote that in the Bible, *name* means "revealed character." So when we pray in Jesus's name, we are praying under the influence of his revealed character. As you become more like Jesus, praying in his name will become more natural, but even then, our efforts to pray like Jesus will be enhanced if we ask ourselves, *How would Jesus pray?* There are many answers to this question, and as you study the Bible, I hope you will discover many of them on your own. But let me get you started.

Jesus prayed *submissively*. Facing the agonies of the cross, he prayed, "Not as I will, but as you will" (Matt. 26:39). That is always to be our attitude when we pray. We are not demanding; we are asking.

Jesus prayed *earnestly*. "In the days of his flesh, Jesus offered up prayers and supplications, with loud cries and tears, to him who was able to save him from death" (Heb. 5:7). Can you imagine what it would have been like to hear Jesus praying with such passion? What a rebuke this is to our cold, heartless prayers.

Jesus prayed *reverently*. "He was heard because of his reverence" (Heb. 5:7). Do not forget that true religion is summarized as "the fear of the Lord." You may pray in a variety of physical postures, but in your heart always be kneeling.

Jesus prayed *privately*. Sometimes he prayed all night, and surely one of the reasons for this was that he might pray without distraction. We need to pray privately for the same reason, and we have the further need to avoid the temptation to show off.

We Are Coming to God for Christ

Are you familiar with Isaac Watts's hymn that begins, "Jesus shall reign where'er the sun"? It is one of my favorites. In the edited version that appears in most hymn books, there is a stanza that starts with this line: "To him shall endless prayer be made." Those are not the original words. Watts originally wrote not "*To* him" but "*For* him shall endless prayer be made." The editors of our modern version thought they were making an improvement on Watts, but in this line, Watts is paraphrasing Psalm 72:15, which says, "May prayer be made for him continually, and blessings invoked for him all the day!"

Now, I understand the discomfort that made the editors of the hymn uneasy with the idea that people on earth would pray for Christ in heaven as he reigns. What could we possibly pray for him? He already is "appointed the heir of all things" (Heb. 1:2). Yes, he is appointed the heir, but he has not yet gained possession of all that is coming to him. The Father has said to him, "Ask of me, and I will make the nations your heritage, and the ends of the earth your possession" (Ps. 2:8). The nations, as well as the ends of the earth, are promised to him, but he has not yet taken full possession. His kingdom is advancing like yeast in bread dough. It started small, but it is growing like a mustard plant from a tiny seed. When we pray for Christ's kingdom to advance, we are sharing in the work. He is administering his kingdom from heaven, and he has left us to carry on his work on earth. He is representing us in heaven, and we have the honor of representing him on earth.

"We are ambassadors for Christ" (2 Cor. 5:20). Jesus was sent and authorized to do the Father's will; we have been sent and authorized to do Christ's will. Jesus prayed, "As you sent me into the world, so I have sent them into the world" (John 17:18). Jesus was sent into the world to bring glory to his Father, not himself, and he described this as coming in his Father's name: "I have come in my Father's name, and you do not receive me. If another comes in his own name, you will receive him. How can you believe, when you receive glory from one another and do not seek the glory that comes from the only God?" (John 5:43–44). When we pray in Jesus's name, we are seeking the furtherance of his kingdom on earth and the glory of his name—we are praying on his behalf about the interests of his kingdom.

We pray as his representatives on earth, and as such we ask ourselves, *If Jesus were here, what would he pray for in this situation?* It is not always possible to answer that question with detailed certainty, but in general, as Christ's ambassadors, our primary concerns are those expressed in the Lord's Prayer:

1. We are part of God's family, so we pray, "Our Father in heaven."
2. God is worthy to be worshiped, so we pray, "Hallowed be your name."
3. God is subduing this world to himself through Jesus, so we pray, "Your kingdom come."
4. God is worthy to be trusted and obeyed, so we pray, "Your will be done, on earth as it is in heaven."
5. We are dependent on God for everything, so we pray, "Give us this day our daily bread."
6. We agree with God about sin and forgiveness, so we pray, "Forgive us our debts, as we also have forgiven our debtors."
7. God is in control of all persons and all circumstances, so we pray, "And lead us not into temptation, but deliver us from evil."

These are seven thoughts every Christian ought to think every day.

On Campus & Distance Options Available

GRACE BIBLE THEOLOGICAL SEMINARY

Interested in becoming a student or supporting our ministry?
Please visit gbtseminary.org

www.ingramcontent.com/pod-product-compliance
Lightning Source LLC
LaVergne TN
LVHW041259080426
835510LV00009B/804